Leading apologists for the past era, such as Sumner Welles, John Gunther, and Raymond Swing, have contended that the Yalta agreements would have strengthened peace and world order if only the Soviet government had not betrayed them. Felix Wittmer, by offering an impressive array of documented facts, demonstrates that the Yalta Pact itself represents a betrayal of American principles.

Carefully citing data upon data, the author shows that Yalta is but the climax of a long series of betrayals which started with the recognition of the U.S.S.R., and which stemmed from ignorance of Soviet aims, strategy, and tactics on the part of America's highest authorities. As the pattern of our costly errors unfolds in this historical essay, President Roosevelt and his closest advisers appear unmasked as adulators of a totalitarian monstrosity. When Roosevelt died a broken man, he himself—as the booklet discloses—glimpsed the range and depth of his tragic failure, for which the American people have been paying in blood and money.

By its synthesis of seemingly separated occurrences the book shows how, throughout the years, the Communist world conspiracy assailed and undermined America from without and within. Rather than expressing opinions the author lets the principal actors of the drama and the most salient events of the unfortunate era speak for themselves. The result is a deepened insight into America's number one problem of survival. It is left to the reader to draw his own conclusions.

This little book is required reading for the student of world affairs as well as the student of Communism. Because of its simplicity and inherent dynamism it will appeal to the general reader.

THE YALTA BETRAYAL

The Yalta Betrayal

DATA ON THE DECLINE AND FALL OF FRANKLIN DELANO ROOSEVELT

by

FELIX WITTMER (1902 -)

The CAXTON PRINTERS, Ltd.
Caldwell, Idaho
1961

First printing, 1953
Second printing, 1954
Third printing, 1961

Printed and bound in the United States of America by
The CAXTON PRINTERS, Ltd.
Caldwell, Idaho
94040

TO THE FOES OF STATE CONTROL—
ANYWHERE

(They are the Genuine Friends of Liberty)

Contents

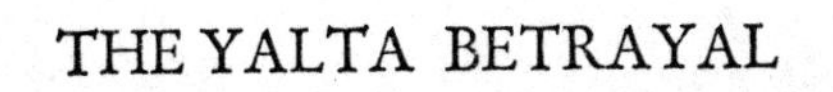
THE YALTA BETRAYAL

1.

Claims and Facts

IN APOLOGY for the Yalta disaster, Sumner Welles wrote of Franklin Delano Roosevelt: "He could not then know that the co-operative relationship with Stalin that he had established would break down almost immediately after his death."[1]

Raymond Gram Swing claimed that "none of the negotiators could have believed that the cold war would be on in three years."[2]

"A bad bargain?" John Gunther asked with reference to the Far Eastern Yalta concessions. "Perhaps it may seem so now. But as of that time, early in 1945, it seemed very good."[3]

Such is the trite and dreary tenor of the writings with which the New Deal-Fair Deal diplomats, columnists, authors, and professors have flooded the land. "Don't blame Roosevelt and his advisers," they admonish us. "Don't blame his followers, and don't blame us who once waxed rich riding the bandwagon. In those days it made sense to trust the Kremlin."

What kind of sense? if I may ask. Such postulates, aimed at preserving a bankrupt administration and saving the prestige of baleful blunderers, are absurd.

Fact is that flirtation with the Kremlin was the fad of tragically ignorant progressives who guided the nation in the years of crisis, and that Franklin Delano Roosevelt, under the continuous influence of the First

Lady, was obsessed with turning his charms on Uncle Joe Stalin.

Fact is that Roosevelt, warmhearted and vigorous, but also excessively conscious of his own importance, surrounded himself with a gang of myopic yes-men who, like Harry Hopkins, George C. Marshall, Joseph E. Davies, and Elliott Roosevelt, frivolously praised the Soviet Union to the skies.

Fact is that the President's Senate-approved cabinet officers often were not consulted before Roosevelt took decisive steps, and sometimes they were not informed after he had taken them.

Fact is that under Roosevelt's monolithic leadership, sensing his determination to establish hail-fellow-well-met relations with the Soviet dictator, the pinks and reds of the alphabet-soup agencies and the legions of blueprint saviors of the world outdid one another in proclaiming the glory of the Kremlin, and that the professional Sovietmongers had a field day that seemed never to end as they took over large areas of our government, radio, and press.

Fact is that the slap-happy indulgence toward the Soviet Union of Roosevelt and his palace guard permitted the cynical conspirators of world revolution to cover our government and industry with a network of Moscow-trained and Moscow-guided spies, to set up an incredible system of fronts, and to infiltrate and corrupt every branch of our public life, including the schools and the churches.

Fact is that Roosevelt, eager to succeed where Woodrow Wilson had failed, dreamed of creating a better and more peaceful world through legal instruments, and in pursuit of his illusions obtruded himself upon Joe Stalin with every imaginable gift, including eleven billion dollars' worth of lend-lease, the security of eighty million eastern Europeans and hundreds of millions of Chinese, and the lives of several millions of the best friends free society possessed.

Fact is that Roosevelt and his left-wing cohorts ignored the warnings of more discerning Americans, from Robert Lansing and Bainbridge Colby to Herbert Hoover and Douglas MacArthur; ignored the hideous and immoral teachings of Marx, Lenin, and Stalin; ignored the chain of broken pledges, the mass murders in the Ukraine, the trial purges, the slavery in Siberia, and the utter disreputability of the brazen liars from Moscow.

Fact is that Stalin and Molotov could hardly believe their eyes and ears when they first met Hopkins and Roosevelt; that, once assured of their mystic credulity, they played our war leaders for all they were worth; once more pulled the timeworn stunt of 1935-39, pretending that international communism was dying out; masqueraded under the flag of reborn nationalism; staged the publicity hoax of the return to religious freedom; fed us, with the help of scoundrels and dupes in our midst, the humbug of China's "agrarian reformers"; and went on toasting us, signing useless documents, and grabbing while the grabbing was good.

Fact is that no "co-operative relationship with Stalin" ever was, nor could have been, established, and that the Yalta "bargain," whether "as of that time" or as of any other time, to men who can name a dictatorship when they see it, never "seemed very good."

2.

The Roosevelts Take Communism Lightly

NOW, LET US view the record.

On November 16, 1933, when the Roosevelt administration recognized the U.S.S.R., the latter pledged itself to refrain "from interfering in any manner in the internal affairs of the United States." That was less than three weeks after the foundation of the American League Against War and Fascism, the treasonable, Kremlin-directed outfit which in 1937 became the notorious American League for Peace and Democracy. Followed the American Youth Congress, 1934; League of American Writers, 1935; National Negro Congress, 1936; Abraham Lincoln Brigade, with its numerous affiliates, 1937-38; the American Committee for Democracy and Intellectual Freedom, 1939, and many more big-sounding traps for impractical would-be saviors of the world.

Soviet secret-police thugs, in the guise of diplomatic and consular officials, traveled all over the United States to bore from within, confuse, bribe, corrupt, and grab. Soviet gold was offered more openly than ever before. In the most spectacular of early transactions, Elliott Roosevelt and Anthony Fokker, on February 28, 1934, each received half a million dollars for selling fifty military planes to the Soviet government.[4] Ever since, Elliott has loved the Soviet cause.

When, in the following year, the CIO was founded, Moscow maneuvered Lee Pressman, of the old Ware government spy apparatus, into the position of general counsel. In record time, the Communists within the CIO achieved a dominant position. By 1938 a list of 280 salaried CIO organizers, who were members of the Communist party, was handed to the House Committee on Un-American Activities.[5] But President Roosevelt reprimanded Martin Dies, at a *Herald Tribune* forum in New York, for investigating the agitators of CIO sit-down strikes. "There is no one interested in Communism," he told the chairman of the committee on August 14, 1938, "no one at all. I've heard it all my life. There is no menace here in Communism."[6]

By this time Washington was teeming with seasoned Soviet spies, such as John Abt, Noel Field, Alger Hiss, Charles Kramer, Victor Perlo, Mary Price, Bill Remington, Vincent Reno, George Silverman, Nathan Gregory Silvermaster, Henry Julian Wadleigh, and Harry Dexter White. Yet, when in September, 1939, after Nazi Germany and the Soviet Union had become allies, Adolf Berle reported to the President the alarming Whittaker Chambers revelations concerning the spy ring of Alger Hiss, Roosevelt shrugged his broad shoulders and advised him to "go jump in the lake."[7]

It was in 1939 that Roosevelt made a decision which, for a considerable period of time, was to turn the tables of history in favor of the Communist world revolution. Over the heads of twenty major generals and fourteen senior brigadiers, George Catlett Marshall was made

Chief of Staff. Six years previously, Marshall's nomination to the rank of general, upon the adverse routine report of the Inspector General, had been blocked by the champion of anti-Communism, General Douglas MacArthur. The two persons with the most incisive influence on Roosevelt—the First Lady and the ex-social worker, Harry Hopkins—both favored Marshall. Both favored the Soviet Union.

Soon afterwards, confident of his ability to evaluate Communism without ever making the effort to study it, and prodded by his consort, the President exhibited annoyance with the probings of the House Un-American Activities Committee into the "anti-imperialist" doings of the Stalinoid peace fronts. (The Communazi phase was then in progress.) The hostile attitude of the New Deal hierarchy notwithstanding, the committee subpoenaed the leaders of the American Youth Congress, a subversive outfit dominated by a crew of radicals from the Young Communist League.

Their morale boosted by the public support of the First Lady of the land, the young revolutionaries found the hearings most hilarious and did their level best to turn them into a farce. The landlady of the White House herself attended the hearings, and afterwards entertained her young friends in the Executive Mansion.

The First Lady's very close friend, Joseph P. Lash, who in 1937 had described his defection from the Socialist party in the Communist weekly, *New Masses,* through a great part of the hearings made a gay and spectacular nuisance of himself. On various occasions one of Mrs. Roosevelt's star boarders, he was at the very time of these congressional hearings a White House guest. Another officer of the American Youth Congress, Abbott Simon, staff member of the Communist publication, *Champion,* for at least two weeks slept in Lincoln's bed.

In the spring of 1941, the young radicals of the congress, as guests of Mrs. Roosevelt, were regaled with a picnic on the White House lawn. The President, to please his zealous spouse, addressed her maladjusted protégés from the South Portico. When he admonished them to condemn not merely the Nazi regime but all dictatorships, he was booed by the First Lady's guests. Soon afterwards, many of these young folks picketed the White House as representatives of the American Peace Mobilization. Among them was Joseph Cadden, one of Mrs. Roosevelt's White House boarders.[8]

3.

Aiming to Please the Kremlin Man

MUCH WAS forgiven when, on June 22, 1941, Hitler's *Wehrmacht* rolled into the Russian plains. Now Russia was on the right side of the fence. Now it was proper for Roosevelt's pal, Joseph Edward Davies, in *Mission to Moscow,* to pay his "respect and admiration" to butcher Andrei Vishinsky. Freda Kirchwey, inveterate Communist fronter, in the *Nation* of June 28, spearheaded the new drive, opining that our leaders were "too sensitive to the general distrust of Communism and the Soviet Union."

In reality, our "leaders" were fairly quick in obliging the most ardent champions of the Soviet cause. It was in July, 1941, that Moscow learned of President Roosevelt's intention to send one Harry L. Hopkins to the Kremlin in order to "negotiate" lend-lease. Who was this Hopkins? For a number of days, no pertinent information from the Soviet Embassy in Washington was available. Consequently, the Kremlin readied itself for a stiff and prolonged bargaining bout.

Top-notch bargainer Vyacheslav M. Molotov was hurriedly appointed chairman of a committee which was to determine in advance how far the U.S.S.R. might have to go in yielding to American demands. The Kremlin then was willing to permit us thorough inspection of lend-lease distribution on Russian soil, including the admission of American military advisers into the Soviet lines. It was willing to give us concessions for mining manganese ore as well as special privileges in the Baku and Volga oil fields. It was even prepared to give us a solemn pledge to maintain freedom of speech and religion.

Yet, a day or two before the arrival of Hopkins, Molotov—for once all smiles—informed comrades Mikoyan, Vassilensky, Trainin, and Bogolepov that the committee was adjourned for good. "A man at the very highest level of the Roosevelt administration," which means a spy either in the White House or in the State Department, had notified the Soviet authorities that "Mr. Hopkins will demand no concessions whatever. The sole wish of Mr. Hopkins," Molotov assured the tovarisches, "is to ask nothing and give everything. What he wants is to keep us in the fighting—and that is all. Mr. Hopkins is completely on our side and may be trusted absolutely."[9]

President Roosevelt had been fearful that tovarisch Stalin might not fully appreciate his unmitigated good will and might mistake him for an economic royalist. At least, the impeccable record of the former social worker and Works Progress Administrator as a lavish spender of the American taxpayer's money, he hoped, would impress the master of the Kremlin.

The President was happy and relieved when Deputy Santa Claus Hopkins brought the good news upon his return from the social pilgrimage to Moscow. Comrade Stalin had unconditionally accepted our generous offers! "Harry and Uncle Joe got on like a house afire,"

Roosevelt stated triumphantly. "They have become buddies."[10]

In order to safeguard transportation of lend-lease material to Russia, British and Soviet troops late in August, 1941, occupied Iran. Naturally, the political agents of the secret police, the "agitprops" who had graduated from the Lenin Institute in Moscow, came along, to exploit whatever resentment and hostility to the imperialist warmongers of the West they might encounter or stir up. The Tudeh party, founded early in 1942, at once began to plow the ground for the Communist revolts which followed World War II.

4.

Roosevelt's Hunch

HARD PRESSED by the Nazi armies, Stalin put on a show to please his temporary friends from the West. Ambassador Maisky proclaimed adherence to the Atlantic Charter—which hardly cost his government a kopek—but continued to insist on the incorporation of Finnish land, the Baltic States, and eastern Poland. Stalin—for the time being—discreetly ordered the "offensive" pictures of Marx and Engels removed from places which allied visitors might frequent, and portraits of national idols like Generals Kutuzov and Suvorov put in their place. On top of the Lenin Mausoleum, on November 7, he invoked the heroes of Czarist Russia—Alexander Nevsky, Kuzma Minin, Dimitry Pozharsky, Alexander Suvorov, and Mikhail Kutuzov. The tunes of Old Russia acquired dialectic materialist tactical significance. "It is ridiculous to think of Stalin as a Communist," Hopkins instructed us. "He is a Russian nationalist." Thus, it was suggested, we didn't have a thing to worry about.

After Pearl Harbor, we rushed headlong into the adventure of brotherhood with the Soviets. Fronts like the Joint Anti-Fascist Refugee Committee, the National Council of American-Soviet Friendship, the American Committee for Yugoslav Relief, and American Relief for Greek Democracy, as World War II unfolded, assumed an ominously swelling significance. Our First

Lady, whose influence on the Chief Executive overshadowed even that of the lend-spend-crazy Hopkins, figured as honorary chairman of the latter two outfits.

An endless stream of American equipment poured into Russia. Over fifteen million tons of cargo, in more than 2,500 ships, were delivered. Hundreds of thousands of trucks, motorcycles, and combat vehicles, and millions of tons of petroleum products and foodstuffs, bolstered the Soviet armies. "Our policy," writes Major General Deane, "was to make any of our new inventions in electronics and other fields available to Russia."[11] Each month the General received a revised list of secret American equipment about which Russia could be informed.

In addition, with evident high-level protection inside our government, we shipped, year after year, millions of pounds of atomic bomb materials.[12] In 1943 our government issued export licenses for delivery of atomic bomb materials to the U.S.S.R.[13] Restrictive orders of the Manhattan Project anyhow were by-passed by the Canadian Radium and Uranium Corporation, an American firm with the "right" contacts in Washington.[14]

Our "friends," the Soviet pilferers, grew so bold that soon they exported baggage without passengers, in batches of fifty black suitcases per throw. Every two or three weeks another batch of fifty, guarded by armed Soviet couriers, passed through our assemblage and transit base at Great Falls, Montana. One single batch of fifty, later in the war, contained 3,800 pounds of oil refinery maps.[15] Everything, from the blueprints of the B-36 Super-Fortress, which had shown up on

Harry Dexter White's desk in the Treasury Department,[16] to photostats of our confidential reports from the embassy in Moscow, was speeded on to the U.S.S.R.[17]

Roosevelt, the genial donor, on March 7, 1942, issued a directive to every government agency concerned to give priority to shipments to the U.S.S.R., "without regard to the effect of these shipments on any other part of the war program."[18] There was no objection to all this from the Chief of Staff.

In matters of foreign policy, the President worked more and more on his own. "I know," he wrote to the Prime Minister, in March, 1942, "you will not mind my being brutally frank when I tell you that I think I can personally handle Stalin better than either your Foreign Office or my State Department."[19]

Although he hardly needed much prodding, the President actually fell ever more compellingly under the pro-Soviet spell of the Hopkins-First Lady-George C. Marshall triumvirate. In 1942 he still had enough independence of judgment left to decide against the suicidal cross-channel operation which Stalin and Marshall urged. Considering that our troops weren't even hardened enough for the African campaign, Prime Minister Churchill was undoubtedly right when he called the Marshall scheme "the only way in which we could possibly lose this war."[20] Soon afterwards, Admiral Leahy, a patriot with common sense, was made chairman of the Joint Chiefs of Staff and, at least nominally, became Marshall's superior.

Roosevelt, who had not been a student of history, or of Russia, or of Communism, like a wild gambler based his pro-Soviet policy on a hunch, as Adolf Hitler had followed his "inner voice" when he invaded the Soviet Union. "I just have a hunch," Roosevelt told William C. Bullitt, "that Stalin . . . doesn't want anything but security for his country, and I think that if I give him everything I possibly can and ask nothing from him in return, *noblesse oblige,* he wouldn't try to annex anything and will work with me for a world of democracy and peace."[21]

The President did not explain why there should be any *noblesse* in a character who once had organized the mail-coach robbery of Tiflis and, as late as the thirties, through butcher Vishinsky, had liquidated most of his accomplices of the Bolshevik Revolution, almost the entire staff of his army, and almost all of the "Fathers" of the Soviet constitution of 1936.

"If I can convince him," Roosevelt said to Ross McIntire when talking of Stalin, "that our offer of co-operation is on the square, and that we want to be comrades rather than enemies, I'm betting that he'll come in. And," the President added with a grin, "what helps a lot is that Stalin is the only man I have to convince. Joe doesn't worry about a Congress or a Parliament. He's the whole works."[22]

How it fitted into the pattern of the Atlantic Charter that Uncle Joe was "the whole works," Roosevelt likewise did not demonstrate. Nor did he comment on the grin of some fifteen million slave laborers in Siberia, or of more than six million Balts who had been "incorporated," or of the Calmyks, Chechen-Ingush, Crimean Tartars, and Volga Germans who had been given the twentieth-century treatment known as genocide.

"Queer thing about hunches," Roosevelt mused when

talking to Frances Perkins. "Sometimes they are right, and sometimes they are awful."[23]

Whether Roosevelt's Kremlin appeasement hunch was awful will be up to history to decide. That the life and happiness of hundreds of millions, and the fate of freedom and Western civilization largely depended on this man's hunches, there cannot be any doubt whatsoever.

5.

Sabotage Inside the Government

INFATUATION with Uncle Joe, following top-level example, became a ritual in the Washington hierarchy. Thus, General Joe Stilwell, who already in the thirties, as a military attaché in China, had preferred the Communists to Chiang,[24] on January 16, 1942, was appointed our commander in the China theatre. The Advisory Committee on Postwar Foreign Policy, which was set up on February 12, 1942, and whose existence was kept a secret, comprised such stout friends of the Soviet Union as Dean Acheson, Esther C. Brunauer, Lauchlin Currie, Lawrence Duggan, Alger Hiss, Harry Hopkins, Philip C. Jessup, Archibald MacLeish, George C. Marshall, Henry Julian Wadleigh, Henry Agard Wallace, and Harry Dexter White.[25]

On May 19, 1942, pressured by Communist union officials of the American Communications Association, CIO, the executive branch of our government issued the first official order to sabotage the security system which the American people, through their duly elected Congress, had established for the protection of their Armed Forces. On that day, Secretary of the Navy Frank Knox, in his office, informed Rear Admiral Adolphus Staton that Communist radio operators were not to be removed from their ships.

Less than half a year before, Congress, with the one dissenting vote of Communist favorite Vito Marcantonio, had enacted Public Law 351, which authorized the Secretary of the Navy to have all radio operators with a subversive background taken off their ships. Rear Admiral Staton, recipient of the Congressional Medal of Honor, headed the administrative board which assisted the Secretary in executing the law. Attending to his duty, the Admiral had recommended the removal of a number of Communists. Now, in the presence of the Assistant Secretary, Ralph A. Bard, Vice-Admiral F. J. Horne, Rear Admiral T. S. Wilkinson, Rear Admiral S. C. Hooper, Captain J. B. W. Waller, Lieutenant Commander F. C. B. Jordan, Lieutenant Commander F. G. Caskey, and Lieutenant K. Baarslag, the Secretary of the Navy instructed Rear Admiral Staton "that, in the opinion of the President, membership or suspected membership in the Communist Party was not sufficient to deprive a radio operator of his job."[26]

Expounding a memorandum bearing President Roosevelt's initials, Secretary Knox brushed aside the objections of Rear Admirals Staton and Hooper, declaring that the order came from the President himself. Realizing that the presidential command defied the law of the land, he refused to put it in writing. Consequently, the Communist radio operators returned to their ships and Rear Admirals Hooper and Staton were put on the inactive list.

Along such lines of brazen infiltration by the disintegrators of the American way, Duncan C. Lee, descendant of General Robert E. Lee and a member of the Silvermaster spy apparatus, in the early summer of 1942 was appointed confidential assistant to General

"Wild Bill" Donovan, head of the Office of Strategic Services. For double insurance, Maurice Halperin, even though on the secret list of Communist sympathizers, was allowed to stay on the staff of OSS. Because of his access to the secret cable room, he could secure copies of our undercover reports from every part of the world.[27]

Actual traitors were so well entrenched in our government that, instead of being shot, they were often promoted even after our intelligence agents had detected their associations and activities. When official reports on master spy Nathan Gregory Silvermaster warranted his removal from the Board of Economic Warfare, Harry Dexter White, a veteran traitor of the old Chambers apparatus and also special assistant to Secretary Morgenthau, pulled the strings to keep him in his sensitive position.[28] Blind trust of the Bolsheviks, fanciful though it may seem, was the official standard.

6.

Professionals Front for the Soviet Union

IN EVERY phase of public life—in our government, in education, in Hollywood, and even in many churches—the Godless Soviet Union was vaunted as a model of the new "pragmatic" morality. Scores of professors of New York University and Columbia University vied with the Sovietists of Harvard and Chicago and New York's New School for Social Research in championing not merely our "gallant ally," but the equivocal causes of the Communist fronts. Bishops and college presidents presided over banquets and conferences which were sponsored by such flourishing red outfits as the National Council of American-Soviet Friendship. A man of cabinet rank, like Harold L. Ickes, in his emotional shortsightedness, rivaled Vice-President Wallace and the First Lady in publicly supporting the expanding and multiplying Communist fronts.

The millionaire lawyer and amateur diplomat, Joseph Edward Davies, who had been our ambassador to the U.S.S.R. in the thirties, stumped the country in every direction to exhort Americans never to toe the fascist line by indulging in criticism of the beloved Soviet Union. "By the testimony of performance and in my opinion," Davies shouted at a "giant mass rally" which was held under the auspices of Russian War Relief, Inc., in the Chicago Stadium, on Sunday, February 22, 1942, "the word of honor of the Soviet government is as safe as the Bible. . . . The Soviet Union stands staunchly for international morality." Mme. Ivy Litvinov shared the platform with the man whom Roosevelt soon was to send to Moscow on a special mission, and ambiguous Edward C. Carter, manipulator of pro-Soviet intrigues inside the Institute of Pacific Relations, presided.[29]

Somewhat more guardedly, but following suit nevertheless, Under Secretary Welles stated in an official memorandum, published in the *Daily Worker* of October 14, 1942, that our government "has in fact viewed with skepticism many alarmist accounts of the 'serious menace' of 'Communism' in China." Years after the war, Earl Browder, wartime head of the Communist party, was to testify before the Tydings Committee[30] that the China policies of the Communist party, toward the end of 1942, "were in fact adopted by the State Department."

Wild-eyed professors, social-minded pastors, and eccentric artists emulated Roosevelt's favorites in ballyhooing the bizarre merger of tyranny and freedom. Charlie Chaplin, Hollywood darling of the pinko fringe, in the *Daily Worker* of October 19, 1942, raised himself to grotesquely heroic stature by exclaiming, "They say communism may spread out all over the world. And I say—so what?"

As 1942 faded out, even the *New York Times* had adopted the "New Look" toward the U.S.S.R. In a mellowed Christmas attitude, on December 25, 1942, it wondered if the party line was ever again to "pass into a new phase of international materialism" and determined that "the thing is not easy to imagine."

7.

Patient Stalin Versus Impetuous Roosevelt

AT THE beginning of 1943 the first rays of victory appeared on the horizon. In May and June, 1942, the Japanese had been defeated in the battles of the Coral Sea and Midway; the Nazis had been halted at Stalingrad on September 12 and the *Afrika Korps* had been routed at El Alamein on October 23. Our invasion of Africa in November had made it possible for Roosevelt to meet with Churchill at Casablanca in January, 1943; but Stalin, the gangster-turned-statesman, preferred to be wooed from afar.

Cordell Hull, in his *Memoirs,* has referred to no less than four occasions on which President Roosevelt vainly tried to persuade Stalin to consent to a meeting. In the spring of 1942; in January, 1943; in May, 1943; and again in August, 1943, Roosevelt made official inquiries regarding a rendezvous with the chief of the proletarian world revolution, but was rebuffed.[31] After all, the Generalissimo had a war on his hands. A fairy could not have been more elusive than entrancing Kremlin Joe.

Like an impetuous youthful lover who is attracted to an exotic woman of some experience, the Groton graduate in the Casablanca phase of the war betrayed eager annoyance as the enigmatic cobbler's son from trans-

Caucasia still kept him waiting. In the meantime, though, the President was going to show to the Kremlinite, and also to the world, what a mighty warrior he really was. During luncheon at Casablanca, on January 23, 1943, in the company of Churchill, Hopkins, and son Elliott, Mr. Roosevelt expressed the idea of "unconditional surrender" as our ultimatum for Germany.

"It was Father's phrase," Elliott proudly reported, and "Harry took an immediate and strong liking to it."[32] Harry always displayed an immediate and wholehearted liking for whatever idea emerged from the mind of the Boss. Usually it was something "progressive," something almost as bold as what the boys in the Kremlin might have figured out. Yet, though Harry and Joe had become "buddies," Harry had not fathomed Joe sufficiently to realize that the chief of the world revolution would postpone the announcement of such a policy until after the Nazis were routed.

Actually, in his Order of the Day of November 6, 1942, Generalissimo Stalin had stated, "It is not our aim to destroy all military force in Germany, for every literate person will understand that this is not only impossible in regard to Germany . . . but it is also inadvisable from the point of view of the future."

Again on February 23, 1943—one month after Father Roosevelt hit upon the Casablanca notion of unconditional surrender—Stalin stated for public consumption that "it would be ridiculous to identify Hitler's clique with the German people and the German state." The *Vozhd* then was working on Field Marshal Friedrich von Paulus, who just recently had surrendered with more than twenty Nazi generals at Stalingrad. He would not want to stir the last anti-Nazi into resistance against the Allies by any scare talk about unconditional surrender. Later, when the Nazis lay in the dust, it would still be time to drop the mask and proclaim a change of policy.

Thus it was not until February 12, 1945—the day after he signed the Yalta Declaration—that Stalin came out with a statement which matched the rash Casablanca announcement of Mr. Roosevelt. The Kremlinite always knew how to use deception on the grand scale as a major global weapon.

The February 12 (1945) *communiqué* proclaimed the Soviet government's "inflexible purpose . . . to disarm and disband all German armed forces; break up for all time the German General Staff . . . remove or destroy all German military equipment . . . remove all Nazi and militarist influence from public office and from the cultural and economic life of the German people."

As to a policy for 1943, Stalin wished to divide the Germans, not to inflame them to forge unity.

8.

Credulity Triumphs Over Warnings

THERE WERE some warnings on our side. Demaree Bess, in the *Saturday Evening Post* of March 20, 1943, predicted that, irrespective of Atlantic Charter generalities, the Russians, at the end of the war, would seize what they could. Wendell Willkie, in the March issue of *Reader's Digest,* referred to Soviet concentration camps he had seen, and Max Eastman, in the July issue of *Reader's Digest,* at the height of the war, told the facts about Soviet world conspiracy and terror. *National Republic,* our oldest anti-Communist magazine, and the socialistic *New Leader* consistently and indefatigably revealed the folly of our Soviet idolatry.

Such manifestations of common sense were lost in the din of the war and the toasts and the propaganda tornado of the Communist-soaked Office of War Information. Preparing for the moment when the Communist armies would overrun Poland, the Soviet government, on April 26, 1943, with total disregard for our side, broke off diplomatic relations with the Polish government in London. Sumner Welles, on that day, expressed his indignation to Ambassador Ciechanowski. It was, however, not the action of the Kremlin which aroused his anger. It was the Poles who infuriated him because they had been courageous enough to ask the

International Red Cross to investigate the Katyn massacre. It was all "German propaganda," he concluded.[33] The Kremlin could do no wrong.

On May 19, 1943, when Joe Davies was in Moscow on a special mission, Stalin confided that he would not mind meeting Roosevelt—alone. He evidently found Roosevelt more "understanding" than Churchill.

Three days later the boss of all the tovarisches (and all the slaves), with a stroke of his pen, dissolved the Comintern. Venerable Cordell Hull, trying to express the entire world upheaval in post-Victorian niceties, reasoned cautiously that neither Roosevelt nor he himself "could definitely say . . . what the dissolution of the Comintern now portended."[34] Anyone who knew anything about Communism could. Ciechanowski in vain, of course, warned Sumner Welles. George Papandreou, Greece's liberation hero, already in July, 1943, told his government in exile that the dissolution was a fraud.[35]

It was shortly after the dissolution of the Comintern that patriotic Rear Admiral Staton, who had been concerned about the President's efforts to sabotage Counter-Intelligence in the Armed Forces, was discharged from active duty. By that time Counter-Intelligence officers had obtained irrefutable proof that the Communist party had developed an extensive plan to abolish the Armed Forces' counter-subversive system.[36]

Two weeks later, Mr. Garey, counsel of the Cox Committee, House of Representatives, asked the rear admiral to testify on the White House efforts to protect Communists in the Armed Forces. Staton complied, in executive session. Before he could appear in public hearings, Adlai Ewing Stevenson, assistant to Secretary Knox, instructed him that "there were White House orders" forbidding him to testify.[37] Patriots who refused to fall for Stalin's fraud were thus silenced by Franklin Delano Roosevelt and his obedient top-level minions.

America fell for frauds in a big way in 1943. When Stilwell, at the Trident Conference in Washington, denounced Chiang Kai-shek as "a fool and ignoramus," our State Department fell for it. When, on June 24, John P. Davies "reported" to the State Department that the Chinese Communists "moved away" from world revolution, the Department fell for it. When, on June 15, Lattimore the Innocent instructed slick Joe Barnes to replace the non-Communist Chinese of OWI with Communists, OWI—rather willingly—fell for it. When, on July 14, Lattimore's old pal of the Yenan days, Thomas A. Bisson, in *Far Eastern Survey,* called Communist China the "democratic China," our journalists, teachers, and ministers fell for it. When, in July and August, 1943, Chinese Communist hordes—in the midst of the war—joined with the Japanese armies to crush the Kuomintang troops, and the Mao lobby "instructed" America that Chiang was "brutally" attacking the ragged but valiant Communists, America tragically fell for it.

9.

Fear of the Soviet Union

REPLACEMENT of Ambassadors Maisky and Litvinov, who were known as friends of the West, by tough and surly Fedor Gusev and Andrei Gromyko in August, 1943, gave our top-level diplomats the jitters. The Western allies by this time had become painfully aware of several distinct Nazi-Soviet peace feelers. As Roosevelt's wartime consultant, W. Averell Harriman, years later officially particularized,[38] it was, up to Yalta, Roosevelt's principal war objective to keep Stalin from breaking his treaty obligation of December, 1941, i.e., to prevent his negotiating unilaterally with his former ally, our common enemy. How, at Teheran and Yalta, we could trust an ally who, we continuously feared, might at any time quit fighting, Mr. Harriman did not elucidate.

At any rate, at the first Quebec Conference in August, 1943, when elusive Uncle Joe once more was "too busy" to join his allies, i.e., unwilling to make any commitments concerning the fate of intended European satellites, the stewards of future American freedom decided to base our policy on a document called "Russia's Position," "a very high-level United States military strategic estimate."

Russia's postwar position in Europe [the document stated] will be a dominant one. With Germany crushed, there is no power in Europe to oppose her tremendous military forces. It is true that

Great Britain is building up a position in the Mediterranean vis-à-vis Russia that she may find useful in balancing power in Europe. However, even here she may not be able to oppose Russia unless she is otherwise supported.

The conclusions from the foregoing are obvious. Since Russia is the decisive factor in the war, she must be given every assistance and every effort must be made to obtain her friendship. Likewise, since without question she will dominate Europe on the defeat of the Axis, it is even more essential to develop and maintain the most friendly relations with Russia.

Finally, the most important factor the United States has to consider in relation to Russia is the prosecution of the war in the Pacific. With Russia as an ally in the war against Japan, the war can be terminated in less time and at less expense in life and resources than if the reverse were the case. Should the war in the Pacific have to be carried on with an unfriendly or a negative attitude on the part of Russia, the difficulties will be immeasurably increased and operations become abortive.[39]

Whether or not the enigmatically taciturn George Catlett Marshall was the author of the document, he certainly sanctioned it, and his patron-collaborator, Harry Hopkins—Stalin's "buddy"—was the man who took it along to Quebec. Russia was to be "given every assistance," and "every effort" was to be made "to obtain her friendship" because, following the war—thanks to lavish lend-lease and the Casablanca folly of unconditional surrender—she was to play an overpowering role in Europe. The document also suggested that we induce our great Communist friend to participate in the war against Japan, even though Uncle Joe had twice before informed our emissaries—Harriman in August, 1942, and Pat Hurley in April, 1943—that he would do just that.

There, at Quebec, George Catlett Marshall, as he did throughout 1943 and afterwards, opposed not only

Balkan diversions but even a Mediterranean campaign.[40] Whatever might interfere with Stalin's coming seizure of eastern Europe, George Catlett Marshall—and Hopkins, of course—automatically opposed. Whatever operation directed our forces westward, i.e., away from land masses the Kremlin hoped to bolshevize, Marshall and Hopkins championed.

10.

Humbuggery and Thievery

ANOTHER startling hoax which those entrusted with American leadership—ignorant or otherwise—did not evaluate correctly was perpetrated on September 4, 1943, when, after an interregnum of two decades, Stalin permitted his stooges of the Orthodox Church to go ahead and elect a pliable patriarch. America dutifully hailed Communist Russia's "return to religion"; Stalin, of course, merely elaborated a scheme for using the Church as an instrument to mislead the Orthodox millions of the Balkans and to attract the Orthodox faithful of the Middle East to the Soviet cause.

Even circumspect Cordell Hull was by then taken in by the Kremlin's professional deceivers. He literally oozed elation when, in October, 1943, at one of Moscow's tovarisch banquets, the Kremlin boss graciously turned toward him and told him "clearly and unequivocally" that, after Germany's collapse, "the Soviet Union would [then] join in defeating Japan." Hull seemed amazingly oblivious of the fact that he had gone to Moscow "to defend the cause of Poland as he would defend the cause of his own country."[41] When he approached Molotov about this weighty matter, the latter wouldn't even discuss that little item of some twenty million people.

The more he was spurned, the more Cordell Hull talked himself into enthusiasm over the Russians and over his success with them. "Of course," he told Jim Farley at the time, "there are matters like boundary disputes and other matters which can wait until the war is over. On the whole, I feel like the fellow who went in on a flush pot with a lone ace and drew three more."[42]

The *New York Times* hailed Hull "Returning In Triumph," and the ailing Secretary, carefully sidestepping the disgraceful Polish issue, told a hushed joint session of Congress on November 18, 1943 that Marshal Stalin "was one of the great statesmen and leaders of the age." Otherwise noted as an astute and rational statesman, Hull in this instance worked up an emotional prophesy which does not stand up very well. "There will no longer be need for spheres of influence," he told the joint session, "for alliances, for balance of power or for any other of the special arrangements through which the nations strove to safeguard their security or to promote their interests." America, whose sons were dying on the battlefields of freedom, applauded; but there were thoughtful citizens who frowned upon the "greatness" of Stalin as well as the "success" of the Moscow Conference.

While such humbuggery was going on, one night, long after midnight, scientist X read a complicated formula on the construction of the atomic bomb to Moscow-trained Steve Nelson, alias Mesarosh, who handed it to Vice-Consul Peter Ivanov, who handed it to Secretary of the Embassy Vassili Zublin, who promptly took off for Moscow. And when, in the middle of 1943, Major General Alexander Ivanovich Belayev, after an unauthorized nonstop flight from

Washington in a radar-equipped plane carrying several thousand pounds of secret data on American aviation, arrived in the fatherland of the socialist world revolution, Joseph E. Davies—millionaire Soviet lover and Roosevelt's trusted special ambassador—as Victor Kravchenko testified, "with 99 per cent certainty," kissed him in the by then customary affectionate manner.[43]

"In certain respects," Secretary of the Interior Harold L. Ickes told the Congress of American-Soviet Friendship in November, 1943, "we could do well to learn from Russia; yes, even to imitate Russia."[44] Our government, then, was full of Sovietist quacks.

11.

The Balkans for the Reds

AT LAST, after pleading for two years of bountiful lend-lease contributions, Roosevelt was rewarded by the elusive master of all the Russias with the pleasure of a personal meeting. The President, because of his physical condition, had hoped that the conference might be held somewhat closer to home, at least not farther east than Basra; but Stalin, who wanted our armies to stay in the West, was quite emphatic about our President coming all the way to the East; in Teheran, he insisted, the conference should be held, and in Teheran it was.

On his way the President stopped in Cairo to confer with Generalissimo and Mme. Chiang Kai-shek. Stalin, ally of Shinto Japan, would not bother to meet the feudal Chinese reactionaries. Jovially and magnanimously, Roosevelt promised to Chiang the return of Manchuria, Formosa, and the Pescadores; a few days later, at Teheran, smitten with elusive Joe's entrancing personality, he agreed with Stalin that Russia should obtain warm-water ports in the Pacific. That meant Port Arthur and Dairen—Chinese ports—and, therefore, a pledge of honor broken in record time.

Placing more reliance on the Communist secret police than on our own American service, Roosevelt, to protect himself against potential Nazi assassins, followed Stalin's gracious invitation to reside at the Soviet Embassy. Why Churchill might be less endangered, or why the Prime Minister's life might be less worth preserving was not discussed.

The infirm Hull had hoped that something concrete concerning the territorial and political integrity of Poland and the other nations of eastern Europe might be worked out at Teheran. Stalin and Molotov, of course, were determined to side-step such specifications; they preferred to be specific regarding concessions of Chinese land and property, about which Chiang Kai-shek was to be left in the dark.

The primary aim of the Soviet diplomats, however, concerned the areas to which the armies of the Western allies were to be confined. Up to Teheran there still had been a chance for the West in some way to participate in the liberation of eastern Europe. General Mark Clark has assured us that the British, fearing the bolshevization of Europe from the Baltic to the Adriatic, had by no means given up their endeavor to make us realize the desirability of a military thrust into and through the southeastern section of the Continent.

Even King George had made it his business to win over the President to this project, through Mark Clark. General Sir Harold R. Alexander "on several occasions" suggested "to cross the Adriatic and move through Yugoslavia." Explicitly, General Clark stated: "There was no question that the Balkans were strongly in the British mind, but so far as I ever found out, the American top-level planners were not interested."

In order to achieve his aim of keeping the armies (and therewith the influence) of the bourgeois-parliamentary-capitalist-"imperialist" West out of the eastern domain, Stalin commandeered (and relied heavily upon) the support of American opinion makers—the Communists and Soviet sympathizers inside the OWI, editorial scribes of *PM* and other journalistic echoes of *Pravda*, and in general the thousands of our Communist-fronting intellectuals.

Dozens of Communist and pro-Communist newspapers and magazines, 70 per cent of which were of the foreign-language category, ridiculed the idea of breaching Hitler's *Festung Europa* by piercing through the "soft underbelly" as "British imperialism." Such publications as the Finnish dailies *Eteenpain* and *Tyomies*, the Lithuanian newspapers *Laisve* and *Vilnis*, the Russian *Russky Golos* (of that time) and the *Shchodenni Visty* (the Ukrainian Communist daily of the International Workers Order) of New York City, by arousing latent national loyalties for "the old countries" among citizens and non-citizens of more recent arrival, served the Communist internationalist master plan of eventual proletarian world revolution.

When Stalin realized that Roosevelt, who at Quebec still had toyed with the Churchillian notion of some action in southeastern Europe, made the big leap and fully endorsed the Marshall-Hopkins-Stalin version of no action either in eastern Europe or in the eastern Mediterranean, he seized his prey with the swiftness of a tiger. Not only did he treat any talk of Western military forays into eastern Europe as superfluous; he now was bold enough flatly to recommend a "third front" in southern France. The farther west our own troops might be diverted, the better for the cause of the proletarian world revolution.

Operation Anvil, i.e., the secondary invasion of southern France, appealed to Stalin more than he was willing to admit; for in order to carry out Anvil, General Clark's army in Italy had to be weakened, and consequently deprived of its otherwise certain victory over General Kesselring's badly mauled Nazi contingent. Once Roosevelt had actually agreed even to this diversionary measure, any landing of the Anglo-American forces on Yugoslavia's Adriatic coast was out of the question, and the Balkans were safe for democratization in the Soviet style.

"Stalin," General Clark reports, ". . . throughout the Big Three Meeting and negotiations at Teheran was one of the strongest boosters of the invasion of southern France. He knew exactly what he wanted in a political as well as a military way; and the thing that he wanted most was to keep us out of the Balkans, which he had staked out for the Red Army. . . . I never could understand why, as conditions changed and as the war situation changed, the United States and Britain failed to sit down and take another look at the overall picture with a view to eliminating or reducing the scope of *Anvil* if something better was offered. . . . A campaign that might have changed the whole history of relations between the Western world and Soviet Russia was permitted to fade away."[45]

President Roosevelt evidently thought that the British idea of some action in the Balkans rather than in southern France was extremely funny. "Whenever the P.M. argued for our invasion through the Balkans," the magnificent hunch player chuckled as he recalled the Teheran plenary sessions in the presence of son Elliott, "it was quite obvious to everyone in the room what he really meant. That he was above all else anxious to knife up into central Europe, in order to keep the Red Army out of Austria and Rumania, even Hungary, if possible. Stalin knew it, I knew it, everybody knew it....

"Trouble is, the P.M. is thinking too much of the postwar, and where England will be. He's scared of letting the Russians get too strong." Son Elliott (big-money, quick-money), Soviet trader, photographer-soldier and would-be statesman, ever anxious to be included among the so-called liberals, agreed with Father.[46]

12.

The Failure of Teheran

THE TEHERAN CONFERENCE occurred long before Americans were told that the nation's survival depended on a fourth term of the one and only who could "handle" Kremlin Joe. Yet, even at Teheran, Roosevelt was not always master over his mind. "An extremely high authority who may not be identified" described Roosevelt's condition as follows: "The President looked physically tired at Casablanca; but his mind worked well. At Teheran there were signs of loss of memory. At Yalta he could neither think consecutively nor express himself coherently."[47] This was the man who, in the course of a decade, had made it sufficiently clear that advisers of a strong contrary opinion were not welcome. This was the man upon whom the fate of the West mostly depended.

Naturally, the American delegates at Teheran, in unqualified accord with the Marshall-Hopkins document of the first Quebec Conference ("Russia's Position"), did everything possible to please the boss of the world revolution. Germany was, of course, to be dismembered. That a totally prostrate and defenseless Germany would open the gates to the barbarian, collectivist, world-revolutionary flood was not openly mentioned.

Secretly it was agreed to let Russia have not only eastern Poland but also part of Finland, the Baltic States, and chunks of Roumania. It was secretly agreed to support the Yugoslav Communist, Joseph Broz Tito, and desert our pro-Western, antitotalitarian friend, General Mihailovich. Secretly it was also agreed to encourage "people's democracies," which were "friendly to Russia," all along the Soviet boundaries. As everyone knows, upon his return to the United States, Roosevelt told a practically captivated joint session of Congress that no secret arrangements had been made.

At one of the "spirited" banquets the lord of the Kremlin toasted to "unity" in dispatching at least fifty thousand German war criminals before firing squads "as fast as we capture them." (Which, in quantity and speed, would have beaten the record of the Katyn Forest massacre.) Churchill immediately jumped from his seat, vigorously protesting against such an outrage to our Western sense of justice; but genial F. D. Roosevelt, ever mindful of the document, "Russia's Position," offered a Rooseveltian compromise. Not fifty thousand but a mere forty-nine thousand five hundred leading Nazis, he suggested, might be liquidated without due process of law. Mathematically speaking, the President of the United States thus sided 99 per cent with the Bolshevik outlaw and knave against Western decency and justice. Elliott Roosevelt, who had not even been invited but who, on the spur of the moment, had been asked by Stalin to come in anyhow, expressed the hope that hundreds of thousands of Germans would be mowed down in battle. While the Prime Minister fumed and the British guests kept stony silence, Joe Stalin, "hugely tickled" and "beaming with pleasure," rose from his seat to swing an arm around the shoulders of the Roosevelt scion. The hearts of Joe and Elliott were beating in unison.[48]

13.

New York's Pinks Oblige the Kremlin

New York's "inside" and "behind-the-scenes" commentators and assorted vanguard troubadours, who have assigned to themselves the weighty task of setting the proper "progressive" tone for sophisticated Americans, obliged the Kremlin in their own inimitable fashion.

Drawing from that treasure of depth and insight for which the *New Yorker* has long been renowned, Howard Brubaker pontificated in the issue of December 11, 1943 (p. 52): "The Cairo Conference put an end to the old custom of kicking China around. In the future, China will be cast in the role of a star player instead of as the ball." If Roosevelt and Hull, who discussed China with Stalin and Molotov, by any chance picked up that gem of *New Yorker* wisdom, it may be assumed that they promptly entered a chain of activities which ended with a double bromo-seltzer.

Freda Kirchwey, idol of New York City's more impatient world reformers, with her habitual finality informed the dwellers of Park Avenue as well as other Americans in the *Nation* (December 11, 1943, p. 683): "No longer will China, like a very poor relation, be expected to suffer and do its duty, but not to ask for an equal voice in the council of the Allies." As even Miss Kirchwey could not help discovering some day, the voice of Russia turned out to be a bit more equal than that of China.

And the *New Republic*, in whose offices such heralds of Soviet "economic democracy" as Bruce Bliven, Malcolm Cowley, George Soule, Michael Straight, and Stark Young pooled their grey matter to chart the course of the brave new world, instructed wide-eyed Americans, on December 13, 1943 (p. 835), that "the great and shining achievement at Cairo and Teheran was a meeting of minds of the four leaders." Considering that Stalin had declined to meet with Chiang Kai-shek physically, we may be permitted to wonder if, in the inscrutable vision of the *New Republic's* pundits, the minds of the two statesmen possibly met by means of telepathy.

George Washington, had he returned to his country at that time, would probably have been somewhat amazed to see the new-fangled, self-proclaimed "leaders of minds" hailing the "meeting" of minds of the free with the minds of tyrants. Perhaps he would have done something drastic; perhaps he would merely have spoken a few simple words, admonishing our citizens once more to "raise a standard to which the wise and the honest may repair."

While there had been various understandings among the Teheran conferees—about Soviet warm-water ports (at the expense of China) and the incorporation of Baltic, German, Polish, and Roumanian lands in the U.S.S.R., and about the necessity of "friendly" governments along the Soviet boundaries—President Roosevelt was determined to assure the American people that no secret agreements had been made. Before he returned home to tell the nation in one of his fireside chats that Stalin was "truly representative of the heart and soul of Russia" and that we were "going to get along very well with him and the Russian people—very well indeed,"[49] Roosevelt once more stopped in Cairo.

14.

Treason in Cairo and Treason in Washington

HAD THE gentlemen of the President's entourage, as their limousines rolled through the streets of Egypt's capital, searched a little beyond the anticipation of toasts and oratorical fireworks, they might have discovered much to dispel the official optimism of the party. As an example, the Soviet Legation in Cairo, which had been established less than half a year before (as a direct result of our trust-the-Kremlin policy), was at that very time distributing revolutionary literature and sowing the seeds of anti-Western, "anti-imperialist" revolts. Along these lines Soviet legations in Beirut, Damascus, and Baghdad were soon to be opened (in the summer and fall of 1944) and the Tudeh party in Iran, guided by the very Soviet officials who were supposed to supervise the flow of American lend-lease to the U.S.S.R., ever more openly agitated against the Anglo-Saxon "exploiters."

By 1944 Iran's mushrooming, Soviet-financed Tudeh press openly called the British and Americans "fascists," "reactionaries," and "imperialists." Similarly, David Zaslavsky, *Pravda* mouthpiece, on January 5, 1944, denounced as amenable a fellow as One World Willkie as "a political gambler." *War and the Working Class,* in Moscow, on January 15 attacked the Greek resistance fighters under Zervas as being "fascistic," in contradistinction to the "democratic" Communists of Greece. *Pravda,* on January 17, accused the British of attempting to negotiate a separate peace with the Germans. Roosevelt's hymns on "unity" with the Bolsheviks notwithstanding, the war of the allies was definitely on. Only, our "experts"—from the White House to Park Avenue—did not see it.

While the hunch-playing world savior, at Teheran, indulged in grotesque fraternization with the cynical enemy of Christian civilization, Commander Floyd G. Caskey, wartime head of Counter-Intelligence in the Office of Naval Intelligence, by way of duty absented himself from Washington to attend a course at the Advanced Naval Intelligence School. During his absence, anti-Communist records in the Navy were systematically eliminated on a substantial scale in various places.

When Caskey returned to Washington, in January, 1944, the lieutenant commander whom he had left in charge of the Anti-Communist section informed him that, under orders, he had destroyed the entire file of approximately one hundred thousand cards relating to Communists and fellow travelers, known and suspected. Though copies of the cards, in alphabetical order, remained in the general files of Naval Intelligence, the destruction of the centralized Red Desk file virtually terminated that section's work. A few months later, Commander Caskey, whose expert knowledge on Communist characters was now deemed superfluous, was permanently assigned to other duties.[50]

After years of taking ever more potent doses of pro-

Communist injections in daily contact with Harry Hopkins, Eleanor Roosevelt, and Felix Frankfurter's un-American protégés, the President was totally unable to fathom the depth of Soviet addiction to which he had sunk. A slave to the delirious illusion of appeasing the Communist barbarians, Roosevelt himself was responsible for the foolish order of January 1, 1944, which, with the backing of Lieutenant General Joseph T. McNarney, Deputy Chief of Staff, abolished the entire setup of the Counter-Intelligence Corps in the War Department.[51] By the will of the man in the White House, who surrounded himself with pro-Soviet schemers like David K. Niles and Lauchlin Currie, the War Department issued the order of February 19, 1944, which purposely disorganized the counter-subversive reporting system of the Armed Forces.[52]

On May 19, 1944, the day after he learned of a recently issued secret order to destroy the War Department records on subversives, Senator Styles Bridges, a member of the Military Affairs Committee, demanded an explanation from Secretary of War Henry Stimson. The latter, as well as the Chief of Staff, seemed puzzled. Lieutenant General McNarney, Marshall's deputy, was "vague, evasive and obstructive." Bridges told him "he could forgive an officer who makes a mistake or loses a battle, but that an officer who betrays the security of his country should be taken out and shot." That brought McNarney down to earth. He admitted that the order had been issued from his office, but added that it had come from "higher authority."

The following day George C. Marshall, in a "hell-raising mood," demanded that Bridges desist from blackening the reputation of the Army by an investigation. Bridges said it was up to the Chief of Staff himself "to keep a clean house." After much wrangling, Stimson, in a letter of May 27, 1944, promised to prevent the destruction of records on subversives.[53]

It was in the same month of May that Mrs. Earl Browder, a Russian Communist of a most un-American political past, who had entered the United States illegally, was permitted to become a citizen. According to the sworn testimony of ex-Communist Howard Rushmore, State Department and Immigration Service officials insisted that they performed this treason-aiding act upon the urgent requests of Secretary Hull and Mrs. Eleanor Roosevelt.[54]

15.

Henry Wallace, Soviet Asia Expert

DISREGARDING thousands of ominous signs, the Washington bigwigs and their intellectual helpers throughout the nation vied with one another to lick the boots of the Kremlin criminals. Columbia University's Nathaniel Peffer, veteran contributor to Communist magazines and IPR confederate of Lattimore, Field, and the like, in the *New York Times* of May 14, 1944, dished up the old story of China's "agrarian reformers."

Vice-President Wallace, newly discovered Far East and Soviet Russia expert, celebrated July 4, 1944, in Chita, Soviet Siberia. Accompanied by such stalwarts of the Communist-manipulated Institute of Pacific Relations as John Hazard, Owen D. Lattimore, and John Carter Vincent, he then was engaged in an official fifty-two-day, twenty-seven-thousand-mile junket to Soviet Asia and China. In a merry whirl of ballets, operas, folk dances, and banquets the credulous Soviet idolater then fraternized with Sergei Arsenevich Goglidze and Ivan Nikishov, dreaded masters of the Soviet Siberian slave-labor camps.

Even after the completion of World War II, in 1946, Mr. Wallace whooped it up for the beloved Soviet Union in a book, entitled *Soviet Asia Mission,* in which he described his record-shattering experience of personal contact and "inspection on the spot." According to the title page, the book was done "with the collaboration of Andrew J. Steiger." In sworn testimony before the McCarran subcommittee, on October 17, 1951, Mr. Wallace admitted that most of the book had actually been written by Mr. Steiger, a person who has been identified under oath as a member of the Communist party. To Joseph Fels Barnes, Owen D. Lattimore, and Harriet Lucy Moore, all of whom have been named under oath as Communist party members, Mr. Wallace expressed his gratitude for their "invaluable assistance in preparing the manuscript."

No doubt the cows in southern Siberia had much in common with the cows of Iowa. That Henry Agard Wallace is a good man at agriculture and cattle breeding, no one will probably deny. Whether his enchantment at beholding Simmenthaler cattle in Siberia was a sufficient basis for glorifying "the common man" of the Kolyma gold fields and the forced labor camps of Magadan is quite another matter. From the viewpoint of our Republic, at any rate, it may be respectfully doubted that Owen D. Lattimore and John Carter Vincent were especially suited to counsel the Vice-President of the United States of America.[55]

Upon his return from the whirlwind journey Mr. Wallace was hailed by the CIO, OWI, the National Council of American-Soviet Friendship, the American Slav Congress and other mushrooming Communist fronts as a world figure of the century of the common man. Now that he had actually "been there," he felt he could speak with authority. Immediately upon touching American soil, i.e., on July 9, 1944, over a nationwide broadcast hookup he told his people all about his "wonderful trip," the "splendid disposition on the part of Russian scientists" and the "utmost confidence" of Soviet Asia's forced labor bosses "in the leadership of President Roosevelt."

There was, of course, no reason for the NKVD monsters of Siberia's Department of Penal Labor Camps to withhold their confidence from the President of the United States. Mr. Wallace himself explained their confidence aptly when he told the nation: "I found American flour in the Soviet Far East, American aluminum in Soviet airplane factories, American steel in truck and railway repair shops, American compressors and electrical equipment on Soviet naval vessels, American electric shovels in open-cut coal mines, American core drills in copper mines of Central Asia, and American trucks and planes performing strategic transportation functions in supplying remote bases."[56]

Mr. Wallace had not "found" the tons of secret formulae and data, nor the heavy water for hydrogen bombs, which relay teams of Soviet espionage agents, with the connivance of high American government officials, had rushed to the U.S.S.R., through our lend-lease air base at Great Falls, Montana, and, by mysterious clearance, through such ports as Seattle and San Francisco. Had he noticed them, he probably would have been even more ecstatic.

At that time, in 1944, the Institute of Pacific Relations, which according to the Senate Committee on the Judiciary "disseminated and sought to popularize false information including information originating from Soviet and Communist sources,"[57] published a fifty-six-page pamphlet, *Our Job in Asia,* which was allegedly written by our Vice-President. "The Russians," the author of the pamphlet claimed, "have demonstrated their friendly attitude toward China by their willingness to refrain from intervening in China's internal affairs." Some years later—on October 17, 1951, to be precise—when testifying before the Senate Internal Security Subcommittee, Wallace saw himself compelled to admit: "It begins to look, for the time being at any rate, that my size-up as made in 1944 was incorrect."[58]

16.

Soviet Fans and Soviet Spies

MR. WALLACE, who "had been there," had been wrong. It is not recorded that our First Lady of that era, who had not "been there" but who sang the same tunes, has ever recanted her own misleading pronunciamentos of those tragic days. Has Mrs. Roosevelt ever apologized for using her considerable power to bring the composer of the Hammer and Sickle Song to our shores? What else was the protégé of the First Lady if not an enemy of our freedoms?

As a mere matter of routine, Mrs. Roosevelt joined the chorus of the CIO and Wallace and the Communist fronts (which she so zealously supported) in chanting eulogies of the fatherland of the socialist world revolution. "Russia," Eleanor Roosevelt said on August 4, 1944, "gives assistance in providing higher education to all deserving students. It can easily be said," she observed, "that we might borrow from that nation."[59]

And Professor Owen D. Lattimore, that ubiquitous and lofty counselor of the Roosevelt administration, on August 23, in *Far Eastern Survey*—an IPR publication—intoned another little anthem in honor of the Soviet Union's progressive policies toward the minority peoples. Years later, of course, the McCarran hearings proved that "Owen Lattimore was, from some time beginning in the 1930's, a conscious articulate instrument of the Soviet conspiracy."[60]

Yet even Drew Pearson, who kept the crafty and trusted Communist party official, David Karr, on his pay roll, and who, because of his charges of "anti-Soviet bias in the State Department," had been branded a "chronic liar" by the President himself, in his column of March 29, 1944, published a long list of Soviet "slaps" at the Western allies. And on May 4, 1944, Prime Minister Churchill asked Anthony Eden to draw up a one-page paper setting forth "the brute issues between us and the Soviet Government which are developing in Italy, in Rumania, in Bulgaria, and above all in Greece."[61]

It thus seems bizarre that Sumner Welles, as late as 1951, should still attempt to keep alive the legend of "co-operative relationship" between Stalin and Roosevelt, and that Raymond Gram Swing, as late as 1949, should be amazed that "the cold war" was "on" three years after Yalta. Hot or cold, the war was "on" long before the Yalta Conference started; in fact, it had been "on" ever since, in 1917, Lenin of the one-track mind betrayed democracy in Russia.

The FBI knew full well that our war with Russia was "on." Was it too much for our chief policy maker to acquaint himself with the bare facts of betrayal in midstream? To learn how Sidney Hillman's "Comrade Big," Lee Pressman, though "employed" by the CIO, was still placing Communist stooges in sensitive government spots, and how the IPR cabal, on Moscow's orders, stabbed anti-Communist Chiang in the back while he was loyally fighting on against superhuman odds?

But Roosevelt, ever since Teheran, had been a dying

man. A British dignitary who had not seen him for fourteen months was "shocked beyond belief at the way the President had deteriorated."[62] When he saw the President again after some time had elapsed, Admiral King "was alarmed . . . by the state of his health."[63] Mme. Chiang was "shocked by the President's looks."[64] Henry L. Stimson was "much troubled by the President's physical condition."[65] James F. Byrnes was "disturbed by his appearance."[66] James A. Farley received reports from "hundreds of persons, high and low . . . that he looked bad, his mind wandered, his hands shook, his jaw sagged, and he tired easily."[67] About one third of the crucial year of 1944—the year in which America did not want to change horses in midstream—Roosevelt was away from the White House, trying to regain strength. Seven specialists were attending him in the spring of 1944.

The President was recuperating at Hobcaw Barony, South Carolina, when in April, 1944, the atomic spy, Clarence Hiskey, approached John Hitchcock Chapin in an attempt to secure a new contact with Metallurgical Laboratories for the Kremlin's ace agent, Arthur Alexandrovich Adams. By doctor's orders, Mr. Roosevelt was on a four-hour working day when, in October, Adams entered the automobile of New York Vice-Consul Pavel Mikhailov, shortly before he vanished forever, after six years of guiding high-treason activities in the United States. Did the President suffer from one of his cerebral occlusions when, in 1944, the FBI was able to reproduce incontrovertible evidence that Adams possessed the most secret data on the atomic plant at Oak Ridge, Tennessee? Was it too much for our Chief of State, who suffered from arteriosclerosis and a heart condition, to bother about the national significance of the meeting of Martin David Kamen, of Berkeley's radiation laboratories, with Vice-Consul Gregory Kheifets (of the Soviet office in San Francisco) who, on July 1, accepted from him classified information on the uranium pile, only to depart three days later for the fatherland of world revolutionary socialism?[68]

Was it too much for the President, who more and more frequently experienced comatose lapses, to learn that the sinister Morgenthau Plan was devised by none other than Harry Dexter White, assistant to the Secretary of the Treasury and at the same time obedient tool of Nathan Gregory Silvermaster's spy apparatus?

Here was the crowning glory of Moscow's brazen treachery, and the tragic irony of President Roosevelt's appeasement gamble. A plain common traitor—highly esteemed by Secretary Morgenthau—was the principal author of the criminal policy which was to "reduce Germany to a country primarily agricultural and pastoral," to "close down the Ruhr areas," flood her mines, have our own occupation forces withdrawn, and have Germany policed by Russian and, mainly, Soviet satellite armies. How was it possible that the President of the United States, who soon was to campaign for his fourth term, was "frankly staggered" and "had no idea how he could have initialed this: that he had evidently done it without much thought"?[69] Was this the man who felt a compulsion to become President just once more, to save America and the world?

While this macabre situation prevailed, the Soviet

government—long before Yalta—betrayed the world of the free in China, Italy, Poland, Roumania, Yugoslavia, Bulgaria, Greece and, with her legions of agents and dupes, right here in the United States of America.

17.

The Kremlin Moves in Italy, Poland, and Roumania

JUST TWO days after we had intimated that, in deference to democratic standards, we would not recognize the Badoglio government in Italy—the savage conqueror of Ethiopia had been rather close to Mussolini for some time—Marshal Badoglio, on March 13, 1944, announced that he and Stalin had agreed to exchange ambassadors. It sounded pitiful when, on March 17, Cordell Hull—who in November had so triumphantly orated on "unity"—let it be known that he had asked the government of the U.S.S.R. for "an explanation of its unilateral action." Molotov was not interested in such trivialities. Palmiro Togliatti, leader of the Communist party of Italy, immediately returned from Moscow, with a host of graduates of the Lenin Institute, to prepare the peninsula for the Communist seizure. By April 21 Communist Togliatti was minister in a "democratized" Badoglio cabinet.

While the three Roosevelts, Hopkins, Marshall, Wallace, Ickes, the OWI, and the busy scribes and commentators were plugging the Moscow line, the Kremlin ruthlessly crushed heroic Poland, for whose liberty His Britannic Majesty's Government, in September, 1939, had gone to war. "The time of liberation is at hand! Poles, to arms! There is not a moment to lose!" Thus the Soviet Polish radio in Moscow on July 29, 1944, at eight-fifteen in the evening. Then the Polish resistance fighters rose. But the Russians, for sixty-three days, denying they knew anything about it, refused to drop weapons and food and so caused the flower of the champions of liberty inside Poland to be massacred by the half-crazed though methodical Germans. At the very time at which Prime Minister Mikolajczyk flew to Moscow, the Kremlin cynically "recognized" the puppet it had set up (the Lublin Committee) as the new Polish "people's government."[70]

While Roumania, through contacts in Cairo, Ankara, and Madrid, was frantically imploring the West to save her from the onrushing collectivist hordes, Anthony Eden assured the Turkish foreign minister "that the Soviet leaders had radically changed their natures, that they had gone democratic and could now be trusted." And our own Office of War Information, which was honeycombed with alien and native Communists, praised Russia's "new democracy" and the "innocent nature" of Communism.[71] The Soviet government proclaimed another avowal of its high moral principles; but by November butcher Vishinsky arrived to "restore internal order."

An incurable League of Nations fan like President Eduard Benes, when finally (in March, 1945) and hurriedly signing a Russo-Czech pact of friendship (of the suicidal "United Front" variety), in all probability acted in comparative good faith; but the British statesmen, when yielding to Soviet intransigence, must have known that eastern Europe was headed for a blood bath in which their very friends—the conscious advocates of individual liberty—were going to perish. Deep in their hearts they must have known that the Yalta Conference, for which they were getting ready, would be another and more ghastly Munich.

There is an excuse for the British which, at that, they might be loath to admit. President Roosevelt, by dint of America's industrial superiority, had become the supreme and decisive diplomatic exponent of Western civilization. Therefore, once Roosevelt and Stalin were in agreement, Churchill—for the sake of harmony and unity—had grudgingly to submit and—for the sake of appearance—had to talk as if the situation were not really quite so bad.

In fact, even shortly before Yalta Harry Hopkins confided to Elliott Roosevelt that the P.M. had "another southern invasion up his sleeve." The two New Deal characters "smiled over this latest effort to get Allied soldiers into the Balkans ahead of the Russians."[72] From the Soviet point of view, there was good reason to smile; for the Kremlin had by then won that fateful political battle 100 per cent.

It was rather pitiful to observe Churchill, by then bickering for the very spheres of influence which Cordell Hull, but a few months earlier, in his "triumphant" address before the joint session of Congress, had declared dead and buried forever. Could we get as much as 50 per cent influence in Yugoslavia? Or perhaps 40 per cent? Or at least 25 per cent? If the Russians were to take over Bulgaria, was it not fair that we assert our influence in Greece? In other words, if the Communists in Bulgaria and Yugoslavia were to lay low the bourgeois lovers of parliamentary procedures, might it not be a fair deal to keep British troops in readiness for any possible skirmishes with the Moscow-supported Greek guerrillas?

The Moscow high command of world revolution was entirely willing to let the Right Honorable Winston Spencer Churchill, as well as Mr. Eden, keep face. It did not alter the realities of eastern Europe one iota, however, when the Prime Minister, as late as December 15, 1944, told the House of Commons: "We still recognize the Polish Government in London as the Government of Poland, as we have done since they reached our shores in the early part of this war."

18.

Double-Talk to Keep Us Paralyzed

As to the position of the Soviet conspirators in the coming postwar world, what mattered was to keep Roosevelt and American public opinion in line. The Communist party and the Communist-fronting liberals of the arts and professions had done mighty fine spade work for that Kremlin effort. The fact that Roosevelt, Hopkins and Hull (the latter resigning in November, 1944) were sick to death also played straight into the hands of the Soviet Union's political strategists.

In accordance with the official Marxist-Leninist doctrine of temporary compromise with the "complex and whimsical zigzag of history," it was now necessary to hold off the Americans just long enough to let eastern Europe be occupied by Soviet soldiers. Once that amazing *fait accompli* was established, the Kremlin might concentrate on fooling them in another part of the world—the Far East.

For the time being, in the period preceding the Yalta Conference, Roosevelt and the Americans were to be kept in ignorance with regard to Soviet long-range plans. They were to persist in their lovely slumber dream and to hope that some sort of friendship with the "vigorous, new economic democracy" of our "gallant ally" would become the basis for future world peace.

Thus the obsession of Roosevelt and the fervent prayer of millions of high-minded but world politically naïve Americans—the honest hope for peace—became America's weakness and Soviet Russia's strength in a game in which the participants played for entirely different stakes.

The trite and mendacious siren song of living peacefully "side by side," played in the thirties for Roy Howard, Harold Stassen, and other Americans who were willing to listen, was now to be offered in brass-enriched, deafening orchestration. It was now necessary for the tacticians of dialectic materialism to make Americans believe that Communism was definitely, finally, and irrevocably dead.

Consequently, such old reliables of the Soviet lecture stables as loquacious busybody Joseph Edward Davies, Earl Browder, and the paid agent, "Czarist General" Victor A. Yakhontoff, renewed their platform antics to make Americans toe the line. Such centers of political confusion and degeneracy as the National Lawyers' Guild, Russian War Relief, and the National Council of American-Soviet Friendship, through the distribution of films, books, pamphlets, and magazines, as well as by sending out expert speakers "free of charge" and by staging "patriotic" rallies, managed to convince Americans that the Russian Bear had turned into a snow-white dove.

19.

Magic Turns Party into Picnic Club

THE HOAX was officially launched on May 25, 1944—twelve days prior to the invasion of Normandy—when at a jumbo rally in New York's Madison Square Garden Earl Browder moved, was seconded, and was unanimously so ordered to dissolve the Communist party. Banners hailing "Our Soviet Friends" and the "Democratic Coalition" set the tone.

Comrade Browder, who now became Brother Browder, announced the birth of the "Communist Political Association," which he described as "a non-party organization of the American working class dedicated to the traditions of Washington, Jefferson, Paine, Jackson, and Lincoln, under the changed conditions of modern industrial society."[73] Therefore, what could be more "democratic," patriotic, and "American" than to join that innocent picnic club of the "new economic democrats," e.g., the Communist Political Association?

Could anyone envisage Raissa Browder's husband as a "democrat"? You could not? Now you see him, now you don't. When the war was over, and most men of character, intelligence, and other leadership qualities in eastern Europe had been put six feet or less underground, bourgeois Brother Browder was to be expelled as a betrayer of the "principles" of the proletarian world revolution. It would, of course, be a cardinal crime against dialectic materialism and the new people's society ever to let any sentiment of any kind interfere with the strategy and tactics of the Soviet high command. For the time being, Brother Browder served the purpose.

Black was white, and white was black. The Communists were "democrats." Good republicans, worried over the governmental infringement upon America's greatest contribution to Western civilization—our Constitution—were "fascists." The party became a "political association"; the Young Communist League became the American Youth for Democracy; the Communist Workers School, the Jefferson School of Social Science; Marx became Washington; Engels, Jefferson; Lenin, Lincoln. Stalin, of course, merged with Roosevelt into one gigantic mythical, "new democratic" character.

The great Roosevelt, who, more capably than either Churchill's Foreign Office or his own Communist-infiltrated State Department, "handled" gallant Kremlin Joe, now had little time left for such trifles as losing the few million East Europeans who, because of their breeding and background, would be the best guarantors of a civilization of men rather than of robots. Though ever more often talking incoherently and losing himself in a jungle of uncontrolled, reiterative, and embarrassing phrases, he now turned his mind to larger and even more supreme pursuits. Upon accepting his fourth nomination, he went off "to inspect Pacific island bases," which was another way of saying that he was too exhausted to go back to Washington, where the President of the United States belongs. Thinning out rapidly, he had to take another shot at recreation.

20.

Communists Lay Down the Law

HARRY S TRUMAN, whom the kingmakers chose as Mr. Roosevelt's running mate, was advised by the President himself to "clear everything with Sidney." This means that, for the man who was to succeed the President of the United States within less than a year, it was necessary to cultivate the most revolutionary labor leader in the nation as an indispensable measure to obtain the required votes. Russian-born Sidney Hillman had learned on Soviet Russian soil how revolutionary plots are engineered. The CIO, which he then headed, was well known at the time to be controlled by the Communists.

When Harry Truman walked into the smoke-filled room in the Stevens Hotel in Chicago (where he was "cleared" by America's foremost Marxists), the widely known Communists (who later turned out to be espionage agents), John Abt, Lee Pressman, and Nathan Witt, were on hand.[74] Less than three months later, on October 17, 1944, Mr. Truman welcomed "the support of Browder or anyone else who will keep President Roosevelt in office and win the war and win the peace."[75]

Yet it is fair to say that Harry Truman, who as vice-presidential candidate shook hands with the Communist agents, was less of a dupe than his predecessor, the Vice-

President who had made the pilgrimage to Soviet Asia and who had visibly and admittedly enjoyed the company of Siberia's slave-labor bosses. This is the depth to which our government—and a wide segment of the public—had sunk. This is the contaminated atmosphere in which the Yalta pact was to be "negotiated."

In line with the deception which the traitors from without and within, through the White House itself, perpetrated on the free American people, the War Department, on December 30, 1944, issued a secret order which destroyed the official barriers against the Communist traitors in the Armed Forces. It expressly condoned "divided loyalty" and established as a guiding rule that "the subversive-suspect should be given the benefit of all reasonable doubt."

When questioned by the House Military Affairs Committee, which investigated the matter, Assistant Secretary of War John J. McCloy upheld the theory "that a soldier could be 49% loyal to Russia and 51% loyal to America." The man whom years later, in a critical period of the cold war, the Truman-Acheson administration was to send to Germany as High Commissioner, to teach the Germans democracy, did not know that loyalty to America excluded loyalty to the fatherland of the Communist world conspiracy.

In this spirit of utter confusion, McCloy and McNarney subsequently commissioned nine characters who had already been adversely reported upon by counter-subversive officials.[76] And by March 4, 1945, jailbird Browder rejoiced in the *Daily Worker* because John J. McCloy and Major General Clayton Bissell (the senior Intelligence officer in the War Department) had confirmed the information that Communist affiliation was no longer any "bar to promotions in the Armed Forces, especially the officers' commissions and special services."[77]

A few months later, in mid-1945, Colonel Charles A. Drake, on orders, had a crew of about eighteen officers, forty to sixty WACS, and a few civilians work in rotation for several weeks to destroy antisubversive records. This was done despite the solemn promise of Secretary Stimson, of May 27, 1944.[78]

Stupidity, treason, and rottenness had penetrated the core of the American government when the moribund President was getting ready for the construction of everlasting peace. Dumbarton Oaks, with Alger Hiss as executive secretary, appropriately laid the ground. Browder, who in the general starry-eyed delirium of brotherly merger had gone to the extreme of offering to clasp J. P. Morgan's hand (but whom the Moscow high command had already marked for the ax), with bourgeois deviationist fervor cheered the President on.

The day before the fourth inauguration, January 19, 1945, Frances Perkins, who worshiped the ground on which Roosevelt stood, was frightened by his pallor. "Don't tell a soul," she begged of her secretary. "I can't stand it. The President looks horrible. I am afraid he is ill."[79] Four days later, the man whom neurologists believed to suffer from a cerebral disturbance, boarded the heavy cruiser U.S.S. *Quincy,* for Yalta.

21.

Ignorance and Treason Set Yalta Stage

NOW, ROOSEVELT hoped, he would complete his immortal work, a permanent peace organization, by convincing the Kremlin thug that the President of the United States was a freehanded, noble, magnanimous gentleman. Had he familiarized himself with the background material which his secretary, Lieutenant William M. Rigdon, held in readiness for him and the delegates, he might have doubted the wisdom of gentlemen negotiating with gangsters. (Kremlin Joe certainly had no objection to Roosevelt being the gentleman.) Was the President afraid of looking at the facts? Or was he merely too feeble to dig into them?

"Later, when I saw some of the splendid studies," James F. Byrnes relates, "I greatly regretted they had not been considered on board ship. I am sure the failure to study them while en route was due to the President's illness. And I am sure that only President Roosevelt, with his intimate knowledge of the problems, could have handled the situation so well with so little preparation."[80]

Mr. Roosevelt's hunch and charm, and the competent advice of Alger Hiss, who was one of the American architects of the Yalta pact, no doubt made up for any lack of background knowledge.

Ironically, the American Yalta delegates were even more efficaciously separated from their British colleagues than had been those at Teheran. The British stayed at the old Vorontsov Villa at Alupka, a half hour's drive west from Livadia Palace, where the Americans were housed. The Soviet delegation resided at Prince Yusupov's Koreis Villa, halfway between their guests, symbolically splitting the Anglo-Saxon "axis" in two.

American preparations had been elaborate. Private cable service with Washington had been established; but our cable ship, the U.S.S. *Catoctin,* because of German mines, was based at Sevastopol, some eighty miles away. Our overland cables, obligingly, were guarded by Soviet riflewomen. What gentlemen would ever surmise that women might indulge in a bit of wire tapping?

22.

Yalta Apologias Don't Stand Up

THE FINALITY of the Yalta surrender—in exchange for protocoled promises and United Nations generalities, neither of which the Soviet government at any time took seriously—cannot be disputed. Soviet apologists insist that Stalin had to be coaxed into breaking the Matsuoka pact and into joining us in the Pacific war by our signing away the strategic areas of our faithful Chinese ally; but Stalin, throughout the war, had assured us through Harriman,[81] Hurley,[82] and Hull[83] that he would "come in" anyhow. In 1943, to Hull, the promise had been made "without any strings to it." By 1944, when the matter was again discussed with Harriman, Stalin—encouraged by the unceasing flow of Roosevelt-Hopkins donations — specified his conditions: "provided that the United States would assist in building up sixty divisions in Siberia" and "provided the political aspects of Russia's participation had been clarified."[84]

Chinese history—the knowledge of which would have constituted valuable background material for our Yalta delegates—has taught us that whoever controlled the north finally gained possession of the entire land. It had been that way from Han through Yüan to the Manchu dynasty. Therefore, an American statesman should have done everything in his power to prevent Communist seizure of Manchuria.

Dean Acheson, in the summer of 1951, declared that Russia's participation in the war against Japan was sought at Yalta because "it was the then military opinion, concurred in by everyone, that the reduction of Japan would have to be brought about by a large-scale landing on the islands."[85] As anyone might know, that happened to be specifically General Marshall's opinion, which was not "concurred in" by General Henry H. (Hap) Arnold, Admiral Ernest J. King, Admiral William D. Leahy, General Douglas MacArthur, and Admiral Chester W. Nimitz. Dean Acheson likewise claimed that "at the time these agreements were entered into at Yalta, we did not know whether we had an atomic bomb or not."[86] Yet, Major General Leslie R. Groves, the man who knew, shortly before the Yalta Conference made a special effort to inform the President that the atomic bomb was a 99 per cent certainty and would be ready in August, 1945. Had Roosevelt still been in his pre-Teheran condition of health, he might, in 1945, have familiarized himself with the background facts of which Secretary of State Dean Gooderham Acheson appeared to be ignorant in 1951.

The official, notarized statement of July 13, 1951, by W. Averell Harriman, wartime ambassador to the U.S.S.R., contending that "nothing that was done at Yalta contributed to the loss of control over China by Chiang Kai-shek,"[87] may be termed fanciful. If some world conference, through sheer economic pressure, compelled us to "internationalize" Minneapolis and to grant a lease on Chicago to the Soviet Union, and to have our railroads to these cities "jointly operated by a joint Soviet-American Company," and if this conference insisted that "the pre-eminent interests of the Soviet Union shall be safeguarded," could we then earnestly claim that we still "retained full sovereignty in America"?

It seems somewhat capricious on the part of Mr. Harriman to suggest that Chiang Kai-shek willingly and even happily "accepted" the terms of the Yalta pact by signing the Sino-Soviet agreements of August 14, 1945, which were ratified by Nationalist China on August 24, 1945. What choice did Chiang Kai-shek have? Was his country, geopolitically, anything but a power vacuum? As his lone alternatives lay between the U.S.S.R. and the U.S.A., was it not slightly better to obey the orders of the American President (even though the latter was baffled and ill-prepared to understand Communism or world affairs) rather than embrace Joe Stalin spontaneously?

"The Yalta understanding," Mr. Harriman emphasizes, "was implemented by the Sino-Soviet agreements which, had they been carried out by Stalin, might have saved the Chinese National Government."[88] Can any man who still is able to distinguish between the American and the Soviet way of life believe in earnest that Stalin might carry out any agreement which at the times does not suit the particular "zigzag phase" of the Soviet policy of proletarian world conquest? Only daily injections of Communist propaganda doses, administered by commentators, editorial writers, book reviewers, lecturers, professors, ministers, artists, and other "white collar toilers" could pervert and debauch public opinion to such an extent that Americans in the highest places could possibly take gangsters for trustworthy statesmen.

Had Stalin acted in good faith, he would have advised the President that Japan was already exhausted. As, by virtue of the Matsuoka pact, he was allied with our enemy, his diplomatic spies—of the embassy and the consulates—kept him informed about Japan. In fact, the Japanese Foreign Minister, on the very eve of Yalta, told the Soviet ambassador in Tokyo that a settlement was quite possible. Consequently, our concessions of territory which did not even belong to us, besides being immoral and illegal, were based on ignorance and stupidity. There are those who believe that they were based on treacherous submission to the idols of the Communist world revolution.

23.

Betrayal of Friends and Principles and Ourselves

THE SAME Roosevelt who urged Britain to give up Hong Kong, and who demanded that the French withdraw from Indochina, saw nothing imperialistic in giving the Bolsheviks a stranglehold on Manchuria, the strategically important Kuriles, Sakhalin, Outer Mongolia, and the ports of Port Arthur and Dairen. What a hue and cry our liberals would have raised had it been suggested that some "imperialist" Western power obtain a port or two.

New Deal fan Robert E. Sherwood correctly explains that Roosevelt was "tired and anxious to avoid further argument."[89] Could America and Western civilization afford a tired man to give the key to China to our most implacable foe? ("He who controls China controls the world," Lenin had prophetically proclaimed.) How tired, we may ask, was Stalin? How tired was General Marshall?

To soothe his conscience otherwise, the President insisted on "free and unfettered elections in Poland." "How long will it take you to hold free elections?" he wearily and fearfully inquired.

"Within a month's time," Molotov replied, they could be held.

Polish elections were held on January 19, 1947, which

was twenty-three months later. They resulted, as the whole world predicted, in a resounding victory for Communism. According to Soviet standards, they were "free."[90]

The chief originator of the Atlantic Charter did not even oppose Stalin's insistence on the use of war prisoners as slave laborers. Worse than that, he agreed to have all fugitive Soviet nationals or citizens of satellite nations, including hundreds of thousands of General Vlasov's firmly anticommunist "Russian Liberation Movement" and tens of thousands of PW's who elected to stay this side of the Iron Curtain, returned to the Soviet Union. The President of the United States, who meant to lay the foundation of global freedom, stands thus guilty of contravening the Geneva Convention and conniving in the most hideous of all of Joseph Stalin's political purges.

"With this shameful agreement as their authority," the *Saturday Evening Post* of April 11, 1953, commented editorially (p. 12), "Russian MVD agents strode through the displaced-persons camps after the war and put the finger on thousands who had managed to escape the Soviet tyranny. These miserable victims were herded into boxcars and driven back to death, torture or the slow murder of the Siberian mines and forests. Many killed themselves on the way. Also under a Yalta agreement, the Russians were permitted to use German prisoners in forced labor as an item in 'reparations account.' For such inhumanities there is no excuse."

Secretary of State Stettinius, who had succeeded Hull in November, 1944, cannot be blamed for these tragic blunders; for, being totally ignorant of foreign affairs, he was not meant to be more than Roosevelt's errand boy and a pleasant companion for sharing the joys of diplomatic convivialities. Hopkins, on the other hand, although like Roosevelt a dying man, did get out of bed just long enough to encourage and supervise Roosevelt's quixotic ventures in totalitarian appeasement.

"The Russians have given in so much at this conference," the President's number one diplomacy fancier noted, "that I don't think we should let them down."[91]

In comparison with the human tragedy of handing prisoners of war and political refugees to Communist torturers and executioners, Roosevelt's concession of three United Nations votes for the U.S.S.R.—which, significantly, he kept a secret—though irritating and hardly excusable, was a pleasant gesture. Only Stalin's interpreter and Alger Hiss are said to have witnessed this particular submission of Roosevelt to the dictator's desires.[92] Years later, in testimony, traitor Hiss claimed that "it is an accurate and not immodest statement to say that I helped formulate the Yalta agreement to some extent."[93]

The Yalta Declaration on Liberated Europe is full of the usual high-sounding phrases about the creation of "democratic institutions of their own choice," "the right of all peoples to choose the form of government under which they will live," and the solemn pledge of the three powers that they "will jointly assist the people in any European liberated [*sic*] state."

24.

The Exultant Mood

SHERWOOD reports that "the mood of the American delegates, including Roosevelt and Hopkins, could be described as one of supreme exultation as they left Yalta."[94] How supreme and exultant, does he think, was the mood of Roumania's venerable peasant leader, Dr. Juliu Maniu, when, as a result of our betrayal, he vanished into a Communist jail? Or of the resistance hero, General Mihailovich, when he was executed at the behest of our intermittent friend, Marshal Tito? Or of Jan Masaryk, when he perished by way of defenestration? Or of Cardinal Mindszenty when, in rather prolonged sessions, his chemical components were readjusted to the pattern of a more useful citizen of a "people's democracy"?

How could a great nation like America, which sacrificed so much in every corner of the globe, be guided into such abject surrender and such a hollow travesty of "global unity"?

At home in America, Freda Kirchwey, in the *Nation* of February 17, 1945 (p. 169), raved that "the communiqué issued jointly at the close of the conference is a most impressive list of achievements." Considering Miss Kirchwey's impressive list of Communist fronting it is likely that she has been impressed to this very day.

Yet even the *New Republic*, whose editors, Bruce Bliven, George Soule, Michael Straight, and Stark

Young, were not known for vigorous opposition to the Communist encroachment, in its issue of February 19 (p. 243) admitted that "on the whole, the results at Yalta represent a substantial victory for Stalin."

The *New Yorker's* trusted "progressive" mouthpiece, Howard Brubaker, in the issue of February 24 (p. 59), referred to the Crimea Conference as "a brilliant success" which "delighted the liberty-loving world." Had Mr. Brubaker forgotten Lubianka prison and the sickening executions of even Stalin's closest comrades? Would he regard the slaughter of tens of thousands of decent Balts as "a brilliant success"? Where was the omniscient commentator's foresight? Where his imagination? Was he then unable to envisage the orgies of pillage, rape, and murder which the Communist hordes would stage among those European bourgeois who believed that the property which they had acquired by industry and thrift was their own? Could the clever esthete not foresee the not exactly delightful mock trials which Tsola Dragoicheva's black widow squads were going to stage all over unhappy Bulgaria?

But Mr. Brubaker had always been eager to express in crisp and fashionable phrases what was held to be bon ton in the smarter circles of literary New Yorkers. It may therefore be considered as quite likely that the mouthpiece "hit the spot." Yalta, in the eyes of New York's intellectual vanguard, was "it." If old Europe and China lay prostrate before the "new people's democracy," so much the better.

In exactly the same vein, one page further in exactly the same issue of the *New Yorker,* Mollie Panter-Downes reported from London that "people here...

appeared to be especially pleased by the announcement that the headquarters of the reparations commission would be in Moscow." Who were these "people" whom the London reporter had interviewed? How would these "people" have cherished the idea of doing a stretch of reparations labor somewhere in the mines of the Ural Mountains? And were our sophisticated New Yorkers really pleased to learn that a war which was meant for liberty had opened the gates to tyranny? But "exultation" reigned from Roosevelt, the cheerful giver, down to the most perverted literary wretch of New York's vanguard aristocracy.

Mr. Roosevelt's feverish exultation, nevertheless, must have been of a somewhat artificial variety. Did he put on a show for the world? Or for America? Or for some of the people he knew who could not help raising their eyebrows at Yalta? Or perhaps for his own self, to quiet unpleasant doubts which made him lie awake before it was time to get up?

25.

Haunting Hunches

THE PRESIDENT had been feeling uneasy about the outcome of his world peace gamble long before the Crimea Conference was staged. Indications of the Soviet leaders' bad faith had been accumulating with frightening rapidity. When even left-winger Pearson had found it proper to enumerate the Kremlin's official "slaps" at us, there must have been something wrong with the Soviet attitude.

Is it possible that President Roosevelt had left Lieutenant Rigdon's background data untouched because he feared that the bare facts might weaken his determination once more—in one grand finale—to outdo himself as the genial and bountiful donor who could break any heart, and finally to clinch his long-frustrated pursuit of elusive Kremlin Joe by a spectacular *mariage symbolique de diplomatie?*

What if Kremlin Joe, whom he had so devotedly served, was basically no better than a common prostitute in whose book the word "loyalty" merely existed as one of the tricks reserved for country yokels? What if he—and therefore America—should have to pay the price of folly which thousands of dupes before him, generation after generation, had paid? Was he, psychologically, perhaps on a level with distinguished but romantic fools who, from Catullus to Toulouse-Lautrec, saw their loftiest dreams dragged through the mud because they treated the underworld in terms of honorable society?

"I just have a hunch that Stalin . . . doesn't want anything but security for his country, and I think that if I give him everything I possibly can and ask for nothing in return, *noblesse oblige*. . . ." These words surely must have risen from Roosevelt's subconscious, again and again, to plague him.

Had Stalin ever obliged? When had he disclosed *noblesse?* The thought was maddening. He, Roosevelt, had gambled on the *noblesse de coeur*—the loftiness of heart—of the anti-individualist, anti-heart "Man of Steel." He had attempted to melt the *coeur d'acier*—the heart of steel—of the robber of Tiflis, the five-time convict of Siberia, the man who had coldly purged millions of Ukrainian peasants because they wanted to cultivate their land the way they pleased and bravely resisted collectivization of their farms. . . . Stalin, the knave who had Bukharin, Tomsky, Rykov, Radek, Zinoviev, Kamenev, and most of his other "comrades" broken in prison cells so that they would testify against themselves and be cast on the trash heap of streamlined humanity. . . . Stalin, the fiend who had ordered the "liquidation" of more than two million "deviationists" of his own Communist party. . . .

Fantastic thoughts must have weighed on the mind of the man who had set out to "handle" Kremlin Joe. Long before he went to Yalta, Roosevelt realized that Stalin might not work with him "for a world of democracy and peace." But if that was the case, if Stalin "did not come in" (to use the words Roosevelt had spoken to the White House physician), then the "bet" was lost, then every move he had made on the global chessboard was false, and his entire political strategy, from A to Z, had been based on a monstrous hoax. "Queer thing about hunches. . . . Sometimes they are right, and sometimes they are awful."

26.

Ding-Dong Show to Quiet Doubts

CHURCHILL's words had caused him anguish, on December 16, 1944, less than two months before the Yalta Conference opened. Couldn't the old P.M. ever adjust himself to the new times? Was it really necessary to have told the world the day before that His Majesty's Government still recognized the Polish government in London as the government of Poland, "as we have done since they reached our shores in the early part of this war"?

The President had been frightened then. What if Stalin took up the challenge and told Churchill off before the whole world? The chasm between East and West would be unbridgeable. Yalta would be off . . . would collapse like the poverbial house of cards, before it was even started.

Immediately, on that same December 16, Roosevelt had implored the Marshal-Tovarisch to refrain from any public commitment with the Lublin Poles. The tovarisch had taken his time in answering. Was that romantic wooer Roosevelt getting cagy? Was he getting fussy? Was he writhing under the grip which had been tightened ever since Teheran?

On December 27, 1944, Kremlin Joe deigned to suggest to the impatient capitalist world reformer that he might as well mind his own business. The Groton graduate who had pursued the love of the "Man of Steel" with everything he—and his nation—had, felt dismayed. Was the ground slipping away from under his feet? Was he sinking into a morass of Soviet deceit and trickery and cynical laughter? Had he heard shrieks? Were those the shrieks of the millions of individuals—every one with a soul which the Atlantic Charter was supposed to protect—who were to be cast before the idol of the robot state, as a gesture of good will, a sort of offering, twentieth-century style?

Roosevelt did not wait eleven days to dispatch his reply. On December 29, 1944, in one of his ever less frequent moments of clarity of mind, he sent another missive to Joseph Vissarionovich Stalin. He had felt hurt by the brusque message, he told the diplomatic bride-to-be with whom, symbolically, he was to middle-aisle it at Yalta. The message had "disturbed and deeply disappointed him."

As a reply to that frustrated lover's groaning and whining, the government of the U.S.S.R. ushered in the Year of Yalta by announcing, on January 5, 1945, that the provisional government of Poland, with which it had dealt *de facto* ever since its birth, was now officially recognized. Let Roosevelt make the best of it. Wouldn't he ever grow up? What else did he expect, considering that the Lublin stooges had been hand-picked by the Politburo in the first place?

All of that, let us bear in mind, had happened before the Yalta Conference took place. When, on February 12, the Yalta Declaration was made public, the Lublin puppet boys grew uneasy. Why should their provisional government "be recognized on a broader democratic basis?" Was the West going to play any tricks on them? But Stalin, who had gone through the motions of the *mariage de convenance* at Yalta, calmed the tovarisches of the Lublin "people's democracy" by entrusting his crony and personal representative, Nikolai A. Bulganin, with a special message.

"The Yalta Declaration," Bulganin told the Lublin stooges on February 17, 1945 (less than a week after it was signed), "is a scrap of paper. . . . You will be the Government of Poland, no matter how those elections turn out and whatever might happen in the meantime. Be steadfast and have faith in Stalin!"[95]

At about this time, on February 13, 1945, Professor Arthur Upham Pope, a vice-chairman of the National Council of American-Soviet Friendship and a perennial booster of the Soviet causes, in the *Daily Worker* (p. 7), indicated the right "line" by calling the Polish government in London a group of "reactionaries" and exhorting the future Fifth Amendment Americans to back the Lublinites. The crypto-Communists and other worshipers of "dialectic materialism" in the editorial offices of hundreds of respectable newspapers knew where to look for their cues.

On the same day, February 13, 1945, Senator Elbert D. Thomas (Democrat, Utah), referring to the publication of the Yalta Declaration, exclaimed: "Mark this day down as one of the great days of world history." The Honorable Warren R. Austin (Republican, Vermont), who, significantly, was later to represent us at the United Nations, said of Yalta: "It's the answer to a prayer."[96]

But on February 24, 1945, in violation of the Yalta pact—which had been signed on February 11—the U.S.S.R. indicated her unwillingness to co-operate in the Allied Control Councils in Bulgaria, Hungary, and Roumania, and on February 27, Andrei Y. Vishinsky, in another violation of the Yalta pact, insisted by an official *démarche* that King Michael of Roumania substitute Communists and Communist tools for certain members of his cabinet. Despite these Soviet manifestations of contempt for the agreements which had been signed at the Crimea Conference, Franklin Delano Roosevelt, on March 1, 1945, told a joint session of Congress that "more than ever before, the major Allies are closely united." It must be left to each one of us to conjecture how the President might have felt when our "bipartisan" Congress wildly cheered his optimistic pronunciamento.

27.

The House of Dreams Collapses

THE VERY next day, on March 2, 1945, it was the embarrassing duty of Ambassador William Averell Harriman to inform the man who had gambled his life's work and his nation's safety on a cordial understanding with the directors of Operation World Revolution that the Soviet government declared itself unable to broaden Poland's provisional government. Consequently, a few graduates of Moscow's Lenin Institute who years before had betrayed their country, Poland, by becoming naturalized citizens of the Soviet robot state, as the core of the Lublin government were to represent Poland exclusively before Mr. Molotov, Mr. Harriman, and Sir A. Clark Kerr.

A few days later, President Roosevelt talked to Arthur H. Vandenberg, the one-time isolationist senator from Michigan whom, in deference to bipartisan national unity, he had nominated as a delegate to the San Francisco Conference, where his dream-child, the United Nations, was to be born. Vandenberg had been feeling uneasy about this unity in what might turn out to be a tragic error and "had been making stern public remarks about what he regarded as Russia's sinister designs upon Poland."

Harassed by the organized smear of America's pinko cohorts in every type of public communication and "information," and quite willing to protect the President against any additional embarrassment, Vandenberg had offered to withdraw. "Just between us, Arthur," the President said, "I am coming to know the Russians better."[98] How nice it would have been had the President of the United States known the Russians several presidential terms earlier.

By March 27, in a message to Prime Minister Churchill, Roosevelt confided that he had been "watching with anxiety and concern the development of the Soviet attitude." Deploring the Bolshevik terror and the open breach of the Yalta promises, he stated that he was "acutely aware of the dangers inherent in the present course of events, not only for the immediate issue involved but also for the San Francisco Conference and future world co-operation."[99]

On April 1, eleven days before his death, in a tragically disillusioned message to Stalin, the President expressed his "concern" over the "apparent indifferent attitude" of the Soviet government with regard to "the carrying out, which the world expects, of the political decisions which we reached at Yalta."[100]

Learning of the betrayal of China—which was yet a secret deal—Roosevelt's old and faithful friend and servant, Ambassador Pat Hurley, hurried back to Washington. "If anybody can straighten out the mess of internal Chinese politics," the President had told his son Elliott at the end of the Teheran Conference, "he's the man. . . . Men like Pat Hurley are invaluable. Why? Because they're loyal."[101]

The President could not help admitting to the ambassador that, on the last day of the conference, in a state of utter exhaustion, he had signed the shameful document. His grief and remorse, in addition to his state of health, must have made him look pathetic.

"Go ahead," he told his friend, "ameliorate it or set it aside, and return to the fundamental principles that you have been fighting for, because they are mine."[102]

Soon, indeed, Pat Hurley and other loyal servants of their country, who stood by principles, were to be ousted from the Department of State. The Acheson-Hiss-Marshall-Jessup era—the Truman era—was to unfold. Harry Dexter White, the deceiver and spy who drafted the Morgenthau Plan, in the year of Roosevelt's eclipse was to be promoted to Assistant Secretary of the Treasury. Henry Morgenthau, his boss, whose views so often had seemed removed from reality, on the eve of the President's death, "thought he was quite normal."[103]

Emaciated, pallid, and trembling, the once ebullient donor and magnificent hunch player had come to the end of the road. The illusion to which he had sacrificed the principles of the Atlantic Charter, the lives of free men, and the honor of his country, had vanished in the clouds. Stricken with despair, the President died a broken man.

One question to Messrs. Gunther, Swing, and Welles: Can you really look Americans straight in the eyes, gentlemen, when you still declare that it made sense—as of any time—to "bargain," "negotiate," and "co-operate" with the criminals of the Kremlin?

References

1. Sumner Welles, *Seven Decisions That Shaped History* (New York: Harper & Brothers, 1951), p. 170.

2. Raymond Swing, "What Really Happened at Yalta," *New York Times Magazine*, February 20, 1949, p. 10.

3. John Gunther, *Roosevelt in Retrospect; A Profile in History* (New York: Harper & Brothers, 1950), p. 359.

4. John T. Flynn, *The Roosevelt Myth* (New York: The Devin-Adair Company, 1948), p. 241.

5. *Ibid.*, p. 192.

6. *Ibid.*, p. 193.

7. Whittaker Chambers, "I Was the Witness," *Saturday Evening Post*, March 1, 1952, p. 102.

8. Flynn, *op. cit.*, pp. 253-55; see also California Legislature, Joint Fact-Finding Committee, *Fourth Report, Un-American Activities in California, 1948: Communist Front Organizations* (Sacramento, Calif., 1948), p. 180.

9. Richard L. Stokes, "A Tragic Tale of Lend-Lease," *Human Events*, April 1, 1953, pp. 1, 2.

10. Flynn, *op. cit.*, p. 340.

11. John R. Deane, *The Strange Alliance: The Story of Our Efforts at Wartime Co-Operation with Russia* (New York: The Viking Press, Inc., 1947), p. 49.

12. United States House of Representatives, Eighty-first Congress, Second Session, Committee on Un-American Activities, *Hearings Regarding Shipment of Atomic Material to the Soviet Union During World War II* (Washington, D.C.: U.S. Government Printing Office, 1950), pp. 1156 ff.

13. *New York Times*, December 8, 1949, p. 1.

14. United States House of Representatives . . . Committee on Un-American Activities, *Hearings Regarding Shipment of Atomic Material, . . .* p. 967.

15. *Ibid.*, p. 922.

16. Isaac Don Levine, "Stalin's Spy Ring in the U.S.A.," *Plain Talk*, December, 1947, p. 3.

17. United States House of Representatives . . . Committee on Un-American Activities, *Hearings Regarding Shipment of Atomic Material . . .* p. 1160.

18. Deane, *op. cit.*, p. 89.

19. Winston S. Churchill, *The Hinge of Fate (The Second World War,* Vol. IV) (Boston: Houghton Mifflin Company, 1950), p. 201.

20. Robert E. Sherwood, *Roosevelt and Hopkins* (New York: Harper & Brothers, 1948), p. 590.

21. William C. Bullitt, "How We Won the War and Lost the Peace," *Life*, August 30, 1958, p. 94.

22. Ross T. McIntire, *White House Physician,* [written] in collaboration with George Creel (New York: G. P. Putnam's Sons, 1946), p. 171.

23. Frances Perkins, *The Roosevelt I Knew* (New York: The Viking Press, Inc., 1946), p. 352.

24. Joseph Alsop, "Why We Lost China: I, The Feud Between Stilwell and Chiang," *Saturday Evening Post,* January 7, 1950, p. 47.

25. Alfred Kohlberg, *Stupidity, Treason or Irrationality?* (Los Angeles, Calif.: First Congregational Church, 535 South Hoover Street, 1952), p. 18.

26. Major Hamilton A. Long, *America's Tragedy—Today* (New York: Post Printing Company, Inc., 18 Beekman Street, 1950), pp. 15-25.

27. Elizabeth Bentley, *Out of Bondage* (New York: The Devin-Adair Company, 1951), p. 182; also pp, 263, 264.

28. *Ibid.*, pp. 164, 165.

29. Special report by Conrad Komorowski in *New York Daily Worker,* February 25, 1942, p. 5.

30. United States Senate, Eighty-first Congress, Second Session, *Hearings Before Senate Foreign Relations Subcommittee* [Tydings Committee] *on State Department Loyalty Investigation,* Part I, April 27, 1950 (Washington, D.C.: U.S. Government Printing Office, 1950), pp. 686, 687, as quoted in *McCarthyism; The Fight for America; Documented Answers to Questions Asked by Friend and Foe,* by Senator Joe McCarthy (New York: The Devin-Adair Company, 1952), pp. 36, 37.

31. Cordell Hull, *Memoirs* (2 vols; New York: The Macmillan Company, 1948), Chapter 90, pp. 1249 ff.

32. Elliott Roosevelt, *As He Saw It;* with a foreword by Eleanor Roosevelt (New York: Duell, Sloan and Pearce, Inc., 1946), p. 117.

33. Jan Ciechanowski, *Defeat in Victory* (Garden City, N.Y.: Doubleday & Company, 1947), p. 159.

34. Hull, *op. cit.*, p. 1252.

35. Max Eastman, "The Greeks Knew Too Much," *Plain Talk,* October, 1949, p. 19.

36. Long, *op. cit.*, p. 12.

37. *Ibid.*, p. 21.

38. United States Senate, Eighty-second Congress, First Session, *Military Situation in the Far East, Hearings Before Committee on Armed Services and Committee on Foreign Relations,* Part V, Appendix (Washington, D.C.: U.S. Government Printing Office, 1951), p. 3341.

39. Sherwood, *op. cit.*, pp. 748-49.

40. William D. Leahy, *I Was There; The Personal Story of the Chief of Staff to Presidents Roosevelt and Truman; Based on His Notes and Diaries Made at the Time;* with a foreword by President Truman (New York: Whittlesey House, 1950), p. 175.

41. Flynn, *op. cit.*, p. 345; see also Ciechanowski, *op. cit.*, pp. 233-50.

42. James A. Farley, *Jim Farley's Story: The Roosevelt Years* (New York: Whittlesey House, 1948), p. 362.

43. United States House of Representatives . . . Committee on Un-American Activities, *Hearings Regarding Shipment of Atomic Material* . . . p. 1187.

44. *The Freeman,* June 18, 1951, p. 592.

45. Mark Clark, *Calculated Risk* (New York: Harper & Brothers, 1950), pp. 368-71.

46. Elliott Roosevelt, *op. cit.*, pp. 184-85.

47. William Henry Chamberlin, *America's Second Crusade* (Chicago: Henry Regnery Company, 1950), p. 206.

48. Elliott Roosevelt, *op. cit.*, pp. 186-91.

49. Sherwood, *op. cit.*, p. 804.

50. Long, *op. cit.*, pp. 26-27.

51. *Ibid.*, p. 12.

52. *Ibid.*, p. 13.

53. *Ibid.*, pp. 28-31.

54. United States Senate, Eighty-first Congress, First Session, Committee on the Judiciary, *Record of Hearings Before the Subcommittee on Immigration and Naturalization, September 14, 1949,* Part II (Washington, D.C.: U.S. Government Printing Office, 1949), p. 785.

55. Henry A. Wallace, *Soviet Asia Mission,* [prepared] with the collaboration of Andrew J. Steiger (New York: Reynal & Hitchcock, 1946), Author's Note and pp. 116-39. See also United States Senate, Eighty-second Congress, First Session, Committee on the Judiciary, *Institute of Pacific Relations, Hearings Before the Subcommittee to Investigate the Administration of the Internal Security Act and Other Internal Security Laws,* Part V (Washington, D.C.: U.S. Government Printing Office, 1951), p. 1314; and United States Senate, Eighty-second Congress, Second Session, Committee on the Judiciary, *Institute of Pacific Relations, Report No. 2050, Report of the Committee . . . Pursuant to* S. *Res. 366 (Eighty-first Congress), A Resolution Relating to the Internal Security of the United States, Hearings Held July 25, 1951-June 20, 1952, by the Internal Security Subcommittee* (Washington, D.C.: U.S. Government Printing Office, 1952), pp. 147-48, 191-92.

56. Wallace, *op. cit.*, pp. 187-93.

57. United States Senate, Eighty-second Congress, Second Session, Committee on the Judiciary, *Institute of Pacific Relations, Report No. 2050, Report of the Committee . . . Pursuant to* S. *Res.* 366 *(Eighty-first Congress)*, . . . p. 223.

58. United States Senate, Eighty-second Congress, First Session, Committee on the Judiciary, *Institute of Pacific Relations*, . . . Part V, . . . pp. 1302, 1306.

59. As reported by International News Service.

60. United States Senate, Eighty-second Congress, Second Session, Committee on the Judiciary, *Institute of Pacific Relations No. 2050, Report of the Committee . . . Pursuant to* S. *Res.* 366 *(Eighty-first Congress)*, . . . p. 224.

61. Churchill, *Closing the Ring (The Second World War,* Vol. V) (Boston: Houghton Mifflin Company, 1951), p. 708.

62. Gunther, *op. cit.*, p. 353.

63. Sherwood, *op. cit.*, p. 849.

64. McIntire, *op. cit.*, p. 175.

65. Henry L. Stimson and McGeorge Bundy, *On Active Service in Peace and War* (2 vols.; New York: Harper & Brothers, 1948), p. 575.

66. James F. Byrnes, *Speaking Frankly* (New York: Harper & Brothers, 1947), p. 22.

67. Farley, *op. cit.*, p. 363.

68. United States House of Representatives, Eightieth Congress, Special Session, Committee on Un-American Activities, *Report on Soviet Espionage Activities in Connection with the Atom Bomb*, September 28, 1948 (Washington, D.C.: U.S. Government Printing Office, 1948), pp. 181, 182.

69. Stimson and Bundy, *op. cit.*, p. 581.

70. Stanislaw Mikolajczyk, *The Rape of Poland; Pattern of Soviet Aggression* (New York: Whittlesey House, 1948), p. 70.

71. Reuben M. Markham, *Rumania Under the Soviet Yoke* (Boston: Meador Publishing Company, 1949), p. 169.

72. Elliott Roosevelt, *op. cit.*, p. 231.

73. Angela Calomiris, *Red Masquerade; Undercover for the F.B.I.* (Philadelphia: J. B. Lippincott Company, 1950), pp. 141-42.

74. Kohlberg, *op. cit.*, p. 23.

75. As quoted by International News Service.

76. Long, *op. cit.*, pp. 13, 14.

77. *Ibid.*, p. 39.

78. United States House of Representatives, Seventy-ninth Congress, First Session, Military Affairs Committee, *Record of Hearings, October 31, 1945* (Washington, D.C.: U.S. Government Printing Office, 1945), pp. 963 ff.

79. Perkins, *op. cit.*, p. 394.

80. Byrnes, *op. cit.*, p. 23.

81. Deane, *op. cit.*, p. 226.

82. Leahy, *op. cit.*, p. 147.

83. Hull, *op. cit.*, 1309.

84. Deane, *op. cit.*, p. 247.

85. United States Senate, Eighty-second Congress, First Session, *Military Situation in the Far East*, . . . Part III, . . . p. 1845.

86. *Ibid.*

87. *Ibid.*, Part V, Appendix, p. 3340.

88. *Ibid.*

89. Sherwood, *op. cit.*, p. 867.

90. Byrnes, *op. cit.*, p. 32.

91. Sherwood, *op. cit.*, pp. 861, 862.

92. Ralph de Toledano and Victor Lasky, *Seeds of Treason* (New York: Funk & Wagnalls Company, 1950), p. 108.

93. *Ibid.*

94. Sherwood, *op. cit.*, p. 869.

95. Rear Admiral Ellis M. Zacharias and Ladislas Farago, *Behind Closed Doors; the Secret History of the Cold War* (New York: G. P. Putnam's Sons, 1950), p. 58.

96. *New York Daily Worker*, February 14, 1945, p. 3.

97. Byrnes, *op. cit.*, p. 53.

98. Arthur H. Vandenberg, Jr., "Vandenberg's Private Papers," *New York Herald Tribune*, March 26, 1952, p. 29.

99. Byrnes, *op. cit.*, p. 54.

100. *Ibid.*, pp. 54, 55.

101. Elliott Roosevelt, *op. cit.*, p. 204.

102. United States Senate, Eighty-second Congress, First Session, *Military Situation in the Far East*, . . . Part IV, . . . p. 2887.

103. Letter of Henry A. Wallace to Felix Wittmer, March 26, 1952.

APPENDIX

Excerpts from Documents Relative To Our Yalta Policy, Accompanied by Self-Explanatory Questions

The text of these documents is taken from *In Quest of Peace and Security, Selected Documents on American Foreign Policy, 1941-1951,* Department of State Publication 4245, General Foreign Policy Series 53, pp. 1-18.

THE FOUR FREEDOMS

Annual Message of the President to the Congress, January 6, 1941 (Excerpt)

In the future days, which we seek to make secure, we look forward to a world founded upon four essential human freedoms.

The first is freedom of speech and expression—everywhere in the world.

How free is speech behind the Iron Curtain?

The second is freedom of every person to worship God in his way — everywhere in the world.

How free are the Poles, the Czechs, the Roumanians, the Russians and the Jews of Russia to worship God in their way?

The third is freedom from want—which, translated into world terms, means economic understandings which will secure to every nation a healthy peacetime life for its inhabitants — everywhere in the world.

How healthy is peacetime life in eastern Europe and in Communist China?

The fourth is freedom from fear—which, translated into world terms, means a world-wide reduction of armaments to such a point and in such a thorough fashion that no nation will be in a position to commit an act of physical aggression against any neighbor—anywhere in the world.

How much progress are we making with regard to a world-wide reduction of armaments? Have the peace offensives of Comrades Stalin and Malenkov made any contributions to it?

THE ATLANTIC CHARTER, AUGUST 14, 1941

Declaration of principles, known as the Atlantic Charter, by the President of the United States of America and the Prime Minister of the United Kingdom, August 14, 1941.

The President of the United States of America and the Prime Minister, Mr. Churchill, representing His Majesty's Government in the United Kingdom, being met together, deem it right to make known certain common principles in the national policies of their respective countries on which they base their hopes for a better future for the world.

First, their countries seek no aggrandizement, territorial or other;

Second, they desire to see no territorial changes that do not accord with the freely expressed wishes of the peoples concerned;

Were the Balts permitted to express their wishes concerning their incorporation in the Union of Soviet Socialist Republics? Was the inclusion of eastern Poland and East Prussia in the U.S.S.R. in accord "with the freely expressed wishes of the peoples concerned"? (The territorial change effected by the migration to transcendental abodes which was forced upon entire peoples—such as the Crimean Tartars, Calmyks, Volga Germans, and Chechen-Ingush—was, of course, ex-

clusively the domestic concern of "our gallant ally.")

Third, they respect the right of all peoples to choose the form of government under which they will live; and they wish to see sovereign rights and self-government restored to those who have been forcibly deprived of them;

Did Mr. Roosevelt and the Right Honorable Winston Spencer Churchill vigorously champion the rights of the Poles, Czechs, Slovaks, Hungarians, Roumanians, Bulgarians, Yugoslavs, and Albanians to "choose the form of government under which they will live"? Have "sovereign rights" been "restored" to the eastern Germans?

Fourth, they will endeavor, with due respect for their existing obligations, to further the enjoyment by all States, great or small, victor or vanquished, of access, on equal terms, to the trade and to the raw materials of the world which are needed for their economic prosperity;

Would the Kremlin plotters of proletarian world dictatorship use free trade for anything but our own destruction? Is it then not rather our "existing obligation" to deny free trade to any and all who aid the materialist disintegrators of our spiritual, moral, and intellectual freedoms?

Fifth, they desire to bring about the fullest collaboration between all nations in the economic field with the object of securing, for all, improved labor standards, economic advancement and social security;

Does economic collaboration with Communist saboteurs mean anything less than suicide? Why then not be somewhat discriminating, for the sake of preserving our ways?

Sixth, after the final destruction of the Nazi tyranny, they hope to see established a peace which will afford to all nations the means of dwelling in safety within their own boundaries, and which will afford assurance that all the men in all the lands may live out

What peace has Soviet expansion established?

their lives in freedom from fear and want;

Seventh, such a peace should enable all men to traverse the high seas and oceans without hindrance;

Did it bring aid and comfort to Korea's freedom fighters to let Soviet ships, laden with supplies for the Communists, traverse the high seas and oceans, from the Baltic to the China coast, without hindrance?

Eighth, they believe that all of the nations of the world, for realistic as well as spiritual reasons must come to the abandonment of the use of force. Since no future peace can be maintained if land, sea or air armaments continue to be employed by nations which threaten, or may threaten, aggression outside of their frontiers, they believe, pending the establishment of a wider and permanent system of general security, that the disarmament of such nations is essential. They will likewise aid and encourage all other practicable measures which will lighten for peace-loving peoples the crushing burden of armaments.

Did Roosevelt and Churchill really believe that the masters of the Kremlin, any less than Hitler and Mussolini, would ever abandon the use of force? Did they advance the disarmament of the Soviet Union by letting her overrun the eastern part of Europe?

THE CASABLANCA CONFERENCE, JANUARY 14-24, 1943: COMMUNIQUÉ, JANUARY 26, 1943

On January 26, 1943, at 10 P.M., E.W.T., the following communiqué, cabled from

Casablanca, Morocco, was made public:

The President of the United States and the Prime Minister of Great Britain have been in conference near Casablanca since January 14.

They were accompanied by the combined Chiefs of Staff of the two countries. . . .

For 10 days the combined staffs have been in constant session, meeting 2 or 3 times a day and recording progress at intervals to the President and the Prime Minister. . . .

Premier Stalin was cordially invited to meet the President and the Prime Minister, in which case the meeting would have been held very much farther to the east. . . .

THE CAIRO CONFERENCE, NOVEMBER 22-26, 1943: STATEMENT, DECEMBER 1, 1943

* * *

The Three Great Allies are fighting this war to restrain and punish the aggression of Japan. They covet no gain for themselves and have no thought of territorial expansion. It is their purpose that Japan shall be stripped of all the islands in the Pacific which she has seized or occupied since the beginning of the first World War in 1914, and that all the territories Japan has stolen from the Chinese, such as Manchuria, Formosa, and the Pescadores, shall be restored to the Republic of China.

What use was there in promising Manchuria to China when Stalin did not even attend the Conference? Were Roosevelt and Churchill unaware of the Communist International's Far Eastern plans?

Japan will also be expelled from all other territories which she has taken by violence and greed. The aforesaid three great powers, mindful of the enslavement of the people of Korea, are determined that in due course Korea shall become free and independent. . . .

How much of Korea will be left when the "due course" for her independence will have arrived?

THE TEHERAN CONFERENCE, NOVEMBER 28-DECEMBER 1, 1943

Declaration on Cooperation in War and Peace, December 1, 1943

We—the President of the United States, the Prime Minister of Great Britain, and the Premier of the Soviet Union, have met these four days past, in this, the Capital of our ally, Iran, and have shaped and confirmed our common policy.

How common was the Anglo-American-Soviet policy, considering that none of our troops nor any of our planes throughout the war were ever permitted on Soviet territory?

We express our determination that our nations shall work together in war and in the peace that will follow.

How determined was the Premier of the U.S.S.R. that his nation work together with the nations of "imperialist warmongers" in the "cold war" peace that was already mapped out for the future?

As to war—our military staffs have joined in our round table discussions, and we have concerted our plans for the destruction of the German forces. We have reached complete agreement as to the scope and timing of the operations to be undertaken from the east, west and south.

The common understanding which we have here reached guarantees that victory will be ours.

And as to peace—we are sure that our concord will win an enduring Peace. We recognize fully the supreme responsibility resting upon us and all the United Nations to make a peace which will command the goodwill of the overwhelming mass of the peoples of the world and banish the scourge and terror of war for many generations.

With our Diplomatic advisors we have surveyed the problems of the future. We shall seek the cooperation and active participation of all nations, large and small, whose peoples in heart and mind are dedicated, as are our own peoples, to the elimination of tyranny and slavery, oppression and intolerance. We will welcome them, as they may choose to come, into a world family of Democratic Nations.

No power on earth can prevent our destroying the German armies by land, their

Could Roosevelt and Churchill actually believe that the Soviet Union would be "dedicated . . . to the elimination of tyranny and slavery, oppression and intolerance"? Was their concept of democracy so broad that they could afford to include the U.S.S.R. among the "Democratic Nations"?

U Boats by sea, and their war plants from the air.

Our attack will be relentless and increasing.

Emerging from these cordial conferences we look with confidence to the day when all peoples of the world may live free lives, untouched by tyranny, and according to their varying desires and their own consciences.

We came here with hope and determination. We leave here, friends in fact, in spirit and in purpose.

Were Roosevelt and Churchill somewhat bashful about admitting that Comrade Joseph Vissarionovich Stalin, "friend in fact, in spirit and in purpose," had reprimanded them for promising to China the rightful return of Manchuria? Was Roosevelt embarrassed because his Soviet "friends in fact, in spirit and in purpose" had ignored his pleas for the preservation of Poland, and was Churchill loath to being reminded that England had gone to war to save the territorial integrity of Poland?

At any rate, were the proud generalities of the Teheran Declaration not mainly the transparent concealment of a diplomatic defeat of which the West could not possibly be proud? In the light of this disillusionment, why the Yalta debacle a full fourteen months later? On the basis of Soviet history as well as day by day wartime actions and the one-sided Teheran diplomacy on the part of the Muscovites, had not the Kremlin's friendship "in fact, in spirit and in purpose" become somewhat questionable?

DECLARATION REGARDING IRAN, DECEMBER 1, 1943

* * *

The Governments of the United States, the U.S.S.R., and the United Kingdom are at one with the Government of Iran in their desire for the maintenance of the independence, sovereignty and territorial integrity of Iran. . . .

Did Roosevelt and Churchill feel uneasy over the activities of the (Communist) Tudeh party of Iran, which had been formed soon after Soviet troops had occupied the northern Iranian zone? Did they, against their hopes, subconsciously fear the coming Soviet-inspired "revolts" of Iran's Azerbaijanian and Kurdish populations, and also the Soviet Union's unwillingness to withdraw her troops once the war was over?

THE CRIMEA (YALTA) CONFERENCE, FEBRUARY 4-11, 1945

Protocol of Proceedings, February 11, 1945

* * *

II. *Declaration on Liberated Europe*

The following declaration has been approved:

"The Premier of the Union of Soviet Socialist Republics, the Prime Minister of the United Kingdom and the President of the United States of America have consulted with each other in the common interests of the peoples of their countries and those of liberated Europe. They jointly declare their mutual agreement to concert during the temporary period of instability in liberated Europe the policies of their three governments in assisting the peoples of the former Axis satellite states of Europe to solve by democratic means their pressing political and economic problems.

Were the Prime Minister of the United Kingdom and the President of the United States of America justified in believing that the Kremlin would "concert" its policies in "liberated Europe" with their own? Just what does democracy mean when the leading statesmen of the freest nations deliberate with history's most notorious tyrants to work out "democratic means"?

"The establishment of order in Europe and the re-building of national economic life must be achieved by processes which will enable the liberated peoples to destroy the last vestiges of Nazism and Fascism and to create democratic institutions of their own choice. This is a principle of the Atlantic Charter—the right of all peoples to choose the form of government under which they will live—the restoration of sovereign rights and self-government to those peoples who have been forcibly deprived of them by the aggressor nations.

Did the satellites of eastern Europe choose their own governments? Did the Poles choose the rape of their land? Did hundreds of thousands of Balts plus millions of Poles, Germans, Czechs, Slovaks, Hungarians, Roumanians, Bulgarians, and Yugoslavs choose forced labor in Siberia? What happened to the sovereign rights of Roumania when Vishinsky dictated the formation

"To foster the conditions in

which the liberated peoples may exercise these rights, the three governments will jointly assist the people in any European liberated state or former Axis satellite state in Europe where in their judgment conditions require *(a)* to establish conditions of internal peace; *(b)* to carry out emergency measures for the relief of distressed peoples; *(c)* to form interim governmental authorities broadly representative of all democratic elements in the population and pledged to the earliest possible establishment through free elections of governments responsive to the will of the people; and *(d)* to facilitate where necessary the holding of such elections.

of her government? What happened to the sovereign rights of Czechoslovakia at the time of Jan Masaryk's defenestration?

What (if anything) made the West's guiding Yalta operator believe that the tovarisches of the Soviet secret police would refrain from mass liquidations once they would tackle the task of "establishing conditons of internal peace" in eastern Europe? Was Roosevelt (without quite admitting it to himself) dabbling in "Realpolitik" to obtain the socialistic brotherhood aims of Harry Hopkins, his spouse, and the rest of the White House camarilla? Was he willing to sacrifice the flower of eastern Europe's freedom fighters to the phantom of his peace organization which, by its very origin and charter, betrayed the principles of human dignity? Anyhow, what vigorous measures did the West adopt to "facilitate" those vaunted "free elections"?

"The three governments will consult the other United Nations and provisional authorities or other governments in Europe when matters of direct interest to them are under consideration.

"When, in the opinion of the three governments, conditions in any European liberated state or any former Axis satellite state in Europe make such action necessary, they will immediately consult together on the measures necessary to discharge the joint responsibilities set forth in this declaration.

How are "concerted" consultations by the three governments regarding the fate of Austria and Germany progressing?

"By this declaration we reaffirm our faith in the principles of the Atlantic Charter, our pledge in the Declaration by the United Nations, and our determination to build in cooperation with other peace-loving nations world order under law, dedicated to peace, security, freedom and general well-being of all mankind.

Can generalities cover up specific and fundamental disagreements? What use principles if they are stretched and twisted to fit their deadliest enemies? Is compromise of principles less than betrayal?

"In issuing this declaration, the Three Powers express the hope that the Provisional Government of the French Republic may be associated with them in the procedure suggested."

III. *Dismemberment of Germany*

It was agreed that Article

12 *(a)* of the Surrender Terms for Germany should be amended to read as follows:

"The United Kingdom, the United States of America and the Union of Soviet Socialist Republics shall possess supreme authority with respect to Germany. In the exercise of such authority they will take such steps, including the complete disarmament, demilitarization and dismemberment of Germany as they deem requisite for future peace and security."

The study of the procedure for the dismemberment of Germany was referred to a Committee, consisting of Mr. Eden (Chairman), Mr. Winant and Mr. Gousev. This body would consider the desirability of associating with it a French representative.

How could any Western statesman fail to see that Germany's dismemberment would weaken the Western defense of the free nations and strengthen the expanding Soviet tyranny?

IV. *Zone of Occupation for the French and Control Council for Germany*

It was agreed that a zone in Germany, to be occupied by the French Forces, should be allocated to France. This zone would be formed out of the British and American zones and its extent would be settled by the British and Americans in consultation with the French Provisional Government.

It was also agreed that the

French Provisional Government should be invited to become a member of the Allied Control Council for Germany.

V. *Reparation*

* * *

[Approved protocol printed following paragraph XIV.]

VI. *Major War Criminals*

The Conference agreed that the question of the major war criminals should be the subject of enquiry by the three Foreign Secretaries for report in due course after the close of the Conference.

Had Roosevelt and Churchill forgotten that the Molotov-Ribbentrop pact of August 23, 1939, branded the Communist foreign minister a war criminal, along with the cynical Nazi? Were they unable to foresee that the Nuremberg trials would be turned into a macabre travesty of international law if the perpetrators of the Katyn Forest massacre were permitted to sit on the judges' bench?

VII. *Poland*

The following Declaration on Poland was agreed by the Conference:

"A new situation has been created in Poland as a result of her complete liberation by the Red Army. This calls for the establishment of a Polish Provisional Government which can be more broadly based than was possible before the recent liberation of Western part of Poland. The Provisional Government which is now functioning in Poland should

In view of the premeditated slaughter of tens of thousands of non-Communist resistance fighters of Warsaw, which the Kremlin had arranged and en-

therefore be reorganized on a broader democratic basis with the inclusion of democratic leaders from Poland itself and from Poles abroad. This new Government should then be called the Polish Provisional Government of National Unity.

"M. Molotov, Mr. Harriman and Sir A. Clark Kerr are authorized as a commission to consult in the first instance in Moscow with members of the present Provisional Government and with other Polish democratic leaders from within Poland and from abroad, with a view to the reorganization of the present Government along the above lines. This Polish Provisional Government of National Unity shall be pledged to the holding of free and unfettered elections as soon as possible on the basis of universal suffrage and secret ballot. In these elections all democratic and anti-Nazi parties shall have the right to take part and to put forward candidates.

"When a Polish Provisional Government of National Unity has been properly formed in conformity with the above, the Government of the U.S.S.R., which now maintains diplomatic relations with the present Provisional Govern-

couraged, and which had preceded the Yalta Conference by many months, could Roosevelt and Churchill possibly trust the good faith of our "gallant Soviet ally"?

What happened to non-Communist Polish "fascists" like the peasant leader Stanislaw Mikolajczyk? What became of Poland's "free and unfettered elections"?

Was the hunch-playing protagonist of Western ideals credulous enough to imagine ment of Poland, and the Government of the United Kingdom and the Government of the United States of America will establish diplomatic relations with the new Polish Provisional Government of National Unity, and will exchange Ambassadors by whose reports the respective Governments will be kept informed about the situation in Poland.

that ambassadors could cope with the liberation methods of the masters of Lubianka prison?

"The three Heads of Government consider that the Eastern frontier of Poland should follow the Curzon Line with disgressions from it in some regions of five to eight kilometres in favour of Poland. They recognize that Poland must receive substantial accessions of territory in the North and West. They feel that the opinion of the new Polish Provisional Government of National Unity should be sought in due course on the extent of these accessions and that the final delimitation of the Western frontier of Poland should thereafter await the Peace Conference."

Had not England gone to war to protect the territorial rights of Free Poland? Had not the government of Free Poland rejected the Curzon Line? Is it proper that people die for principles while their statesmen compromise these principles? What, anyhow, has become of that Peace Conference?

VIII. *Yugoslavia*

It is agreed to recommend to Marshal Tito and to Dr. Subasic:

(*a*) that the Tito-Subasic Agreement should immediately be put into effect and a

Considering that Tito was a trainee of the Lenin Institute, i.e., an accredited graduate of the treacherous Soviet secret police, and that at the

new Government formed on the basis of the Agreement

(b) that as soon as the new Government has been formed it should declare:

(i) that the Anti-Fascist Assembly of National Liberation (Aunoj) will be extended to include members of the last Yugoslav Skupstina who have not compromised themselves by collaboration with the enemy, thus forming a body to be known as a temporary Parliament and

(ii) that legislative acts passed by the Anti-Fascist Assembly of National Liberation (Aunoj) will be subject to subsequent ratification by a Constituent Assembly; and that this statement should be published in the Communiqué of the Conference.

time he was in the process of butchering the heroic followers of non-Communist resistance patriot Mihailovich, how much sense did it make to put any stock whatever in a Tito-Subasic Agreement?

Did the members of the last Skupstina (i.e., Yugoslav parliament) fare any better than did the imprisoned Archbishop (now Cardinal) Aloysius Stepinac? And when Mihailovich, in 1946, at the behest of Comrade Tito, was executed, did perhaps F. D. Roosevelt, who had left this earth more than a year earlier, welcome him in another realm with all the charm of his noted broad grin? Or is it unlikely that our Lord called the two figures of the second World War to the same nonterrestrial spheres?

IX. *Italo-Yugoslav Frontier*
Italo-Austria Frontier

Notes on these subjects were put in by the British delegation and the American and Soviet delegations agreed to consider them and give their views later.

Shall the Italo-Yugoslav and Italo-Austrian frontier dwellers have the pleasure of reading many more diplomatic notes while enjoying the thrills of figuring out to what government one of these days they may be permitted to swear allegiance "forever"?

X. *Yugoslav-Bulgarian Relations*

There was an exchange of

views between the Foreign Secretaries on the question of the desirability of a Yugoslav-Bulgarian pact of alliance. The question at issue was whether a state still under an armistice regime could be allowed to enter into a treaty with another state. Mr. Eden suggested that the Bulgarian and Yugoslav Governments should be informed that this could not be approved. Mr. Stettinius suggested that the British and American Ambassadors should discuss the matter further with M. Molotov in Moscow. M. Molotov agreed with the proposal of Mr. Stettinius.

Did Mr. Molotov remember Paragraph X of the Yalta Pact when his government signed an alliance with a quickly set-up Bulgarian satellite government? As to American and British "ambassadors," are they still in the discussion stage?

XI. *Southeastern Europe*

The British Delegation put in notes for the consideration of their colleagues on the following subjects:

(a) the Control Commission in Bulgaria

(b) Greek claims upon Bulgaria, more particularly with reference to reparations

(c) oil equipment in Rumania.

What happened to the notes?

XII. *Iran*

Mr. Eden, Mr. Stettinius and M. Molotov exchanged views on the situation in Iran. It was agreed that this matter should be pursued through the diplomatic channel.

How diplomatic were the channels when the Soviet Union did not wish to withdraw her troops from Iran and Comrade Andrei Gromyko, angered by UN arguments, went for a walk?

XIII. *Meetings of the Three Foreign Secretaries*

The Conference agreed that permanent machinery should be set up for consultation between the three Foreign Secretaries; they should meet as often as necessary, probably about every three or four months.

What has become of the permanent consultations?

These meetings will be held in rotation in the three capitals, the first meeting being held in London.

XIV. *The Montreux Convention and the Straits*

It was agreed that at the next meeting of the three Foreign Secretaries to be held in London, they should consider proposals which it was understood the Soviet Government would put forward in relation to the Montreux Convention and report to their Governments. The Turkish Government should be informed at the appropriate moment.

How democratic, "in fact, in spirit and in purpose," was the U.S.S.R.'s expressed desire to "participate" in the "defense" of the Turkish Straits?

The foregoing Protocol was approved and signed by the three Foreign Secretaries at the Crimean Conference, February 11, 1945.

E. R. Stettinius, Jr.
M. Molotov
Anthony Eden

PROTOCOL ON GERMAN REPARATION, FEBRUARY 11, 1945

The Heads of the three governments agreed as follows:

1. Germany must pay in kind for the losses caused by her to the Allied nations in the course of the war. Reparations are to be received in the first instance by those countries which have borne the main burden of the war, have suffered the heaviest losses and have organized victory over the enemy.

2. Reparation in kind are to be exacted from Germany in three following forms:

(a) Removals within 2 years from the surrender of Germany or the cessation of organized resistance from the national wealth of Germany located on the territory of Germany herself as well as outside her territory (equipment, machine-tools, ships, rolling stock, German investments abroad, shares of industrial, transport and other enterprises in Germany etc.), these removals to be carried out chiefly for purpose of destroying the war potential of Germany.

(b) Annual deliveries of goods from current production for a period to be fixed.

Was President Roosevelt in one of his ever more frequent states of mental semi-paralysis when he consented to the permanent weakening of Germany by way of de-industrialization and "pasturization"? How proud would the veteran hunch-player have been of his statesmanship had he lived long enough to learn that the Morgenthau Plan had been drafted by Harry Dexter White, obedient servant of a Soviet spy apparatus inside the Washington administration?

(*c*) Use of German labour.

What difference has there been between the "use of German labor" and slave labor, Muscovite style? If there hasn't been any, is it not true that Mr. Roosevelt and the Right Honorable Winston Spencer Churchill, by hastily affixing their signatures to the Protocol of February 11, 1945, broke international law and contravened the (humanitarian) Geneva Convention?

3. For the working out on the above principles of a detailed plan for exaction of reparation from Germany an Allied Reparation Commission will be set up in Moscow. It will consist of three representatives — one from the Union of Soviet Socialist Republics, one from the United Kingdom and one from the United States of America.

How do the "above principles" fit into the lofty pattern of the Atlantic Charter?

4. With regard to the fixing of the total sum of the reparation as well as the distribution of it among the countries which suffered from the German aggression the Soviet and American delegations agreed as follows:

"The Moscow Reparation Commission should take in its initial studies as a basis for discussion the suggestion of the Soviet Government that the total sum of the reparation in accordance with the points (a) and (b) of the paragraph 2 should be 20 billion dollars and that 50% of it should go to the Union of Soviet Socialist Republics."

The British delegation was of the opinion that pending consideration of the reparation question by the Moscow Reparation Commission no figures of reparation should be mentioned.

The above Soviet-American proposal has been passed to the Moscow Reparation Commission as one of the proposals to be considered by the Commission.

WINSTON S. CHURCHILL
FRANKLIN D. ROOSEVELT
JOSEPH V. STALIN
February 11, 1945

Considering that at the end of World War II Germany was unable even to feed herself, is it not a fact that any cash payment to the U.S.S.R. meant an additional burden for the American taxpayer?

AGREEMENT REGARDING JAPAN FEBRUARY 11, 1945

The leaders of the three Great Powers — the Soviet Union, the United States of America and Great Britain—have agreed that in two or three months after Germany has surrendered and the war in Europe has terminated the Soviet Union shall enter into the war against Japan on the side of the Allies on condition that:

Inasmuch as, since the Baku Conference in 1920, the conquest of Asia had been the cornerstone of Communist world strategy, was it not the obligation of a wide-awake American government to do everything in its power to prevent the U.S.S.R. from par-

1. The status quo in Outer Mongolia (The Mongolian People's Republic) shall be preserved;

2. The former rights of Russia violated by the treacherous attack of Japan in 1904 shall be restored, viz:

(a) the southern part of Sakhalin as well as all the islands adjacent to it shall be returned to the Soviet Union,

(b) the commercial port of Dairen shall be internationalized, the pre-eminent interests of the Soviet Union in this port being safeguarded and the lease of Port Arthur as a naval base of the U.S.S.R. restored,

(c) the Chinese-Eastern Railroad and the South-Manchurian Railroad which provides an outlet to Dairen shall be jointly operated by the establishment of a joint Soviet-Chinese Company it being understood that the pre-emi-

ticipating in the war against Japan?

Had there not been a time when the Communists of the Lenin-Trotsky-Zinoviev-Radek stripe had denounced Czarist imperialism in the Far East?

How does such surrender to Soviet imperialism jibe with the solemn promises which we gave to the Chinese government at the Cairo Conference in 1943? What right did we have to make a deal with the Soviet Union at the expense of a faithful ally? Why did President Roosevelt and Prime Minister Churchill not avail themselves of the lessons of Far Eastern history and geopolitics which overwhelmingly indicated that whoever controlled the north of China would eventually capture the rest of that nation?

Has any "joint operation" with the Stalinists, unless discontinued in the nick of time, ever meant anything but the questionable pleasure of being devoured by the Soviet Bear? Did the teachings and maneuvers of the IPR at last bear nent interests of the Soviet Union shall be safeguarded and that China shall retain full sovereignty in Manchuria;

fruit? How solidly by then were the Soviet Firsters entrenched in Washington that it was possible for our Far Eastern "experts" to override the will of far-sighted Chiang Kai-shek in advising the suicidal Chinese-Soviet co-operation? Why, it seems fair to inquire, was Roosevelt unwilling to benefit by the wisdom of Chiang, who had experienced Communist treachery two decades earlier (when Borodin, Joffe, Roy, and their ilk infiltrated the Kuomintang) and who, on the basis of incontestable documents, knew of Comrade Mao's abject allegiance to Moscow?

How, furthermore, could China be expected to "retain full sovereignty in Manchuria" once the life lines of that strategic area, by way of "joint operation," were controlled by the Communist world revolutionaries? How, then, was this Yalta "Agreement" anything less grave than a betrayal—of our faithful ally, the principles of the Atlantic Charter, and the boys who died for them on far-flung battlefields?

3. The Kurile islands shall be handed over to the Soviet Union.

Why not supply the world revolutionists with airfields and submarine bases closer to Alaska? How generous can gambling statesmen get?

It is understood, that the agreement concerning Outer Mongolia and the ports and railroads referred to above will require concurrence of Generalissimo Chiang Kai-shek. The President will take measures in order to obtain this concurrence on advice from Marshal Stalin.

And what if Chiang Kai-shek balked? Would he be forced into concurrence (or rather submission) by threats of economic pressure such as we applied in the days of the fatal Marshall mission? And what will future students of history think when they read that the President of the United States, elected by the freest and best-informed people in the world, would admittedly take advice from the mail-coach robber of Tiflis who plotted the destruction of "bourgeois" America, and who ruled over his frightened robot subjects by means of slave labor and execution?

The Heads of the three Great Powers have agreed that these claims of the Soviet Union shall be unquestionably fulfilled after Japan has been defeated.

What chance of "free concurrence" was left to our ally, Nationalist China, if "these claims of the Soviet Union" were to be "unquestionably fulfilled"? Had not Roosevelt and Churchill, on August 14, 1941, solemnly declared that they desired "to see no territorial changes that do not accord with the freely expressed wishes of the peoples concerned"? When did the Chinese people of Manchuria, Dairen, and Port Arthur have an opportunity to express their possible wishes concerning territorial changes and change of allegiance "freely"?

For its part the Soviet Union

Was Roosevelt entirely un-

expresses its readiness to conclude with the National Government of China a pact of friendship and alliance between the U.S.S.R. and China in order to render assistance to China with its armed forces for the purpose of liberating China from the Japanese yoke.

JOSEPH V. STALIN
FRANKLIN D. ROOSEVELT
WINSTON S. CHURCHILL

February 11, 1945

aware of the documented fact that Chinese Communist troops, on many occasions, had co-operated with the Japanese to annihilate Nationalist Chinese contingents, even during the war? How could Roosevelt and Churchill dare to force "a pact of friendship and alliance" on Chiang Kai-shek when the latter, in his superior wisdom, feared nothing more than the Soviet Trojan horse? Was signing the death warrant of a loyal and brilliant ally anything less than betrayal?

Index